PRAYER WORKS
if you work it!

Randal D. Reese

Mansfield, Georgia

Prayer Works If You Work It

Copyright © 2022 Randal D. Reese
Published by Until That Day Ministries, Mansfield, Georgia

ISBN 979-8-9873373-0-1

All rights reserved. No part of this book may be reproduced, stored in a retrieval system, or transmitted in any form by any means—electronic, mechanical, photocopy, recording, or other—without prior written permission of the publisher.

Scripture references are taken from the King James Version of the Bible.

Cover and Interior Design by Katie Caron

Printed in the United States of America

The goal of this book...

is to motivate every Christian
to enlarge his or her prayer life,
and to invite those who do not have
a personal relationship with Jesus Christ
to experience His forgiveness
and enjoy His presence daily,
and to live with an expectation
of answered prayer.

Our desire is...
"Lord teach us to pray!"

CONTENTS

CHAPTER ONE
The Power of Prayer
7

CHAPTER TWO
The Purpose of Prayer
21

CHAPTER THREE
The Power of Prayer and Fasting
31

CHAPTER FOUR
The Practice of Prayer: Daily Devotionals
35

CHAPTER FIVE
The Intercessor's Prayer
125

Conclusion
129

Appendix: A Legacy of Prayer and Fasting 131
Notes 135
Author 137

CHAPTER ONE
THE POWER OF PRAYER

*"Let us therefore come boldly
unto the throne of grace,
that we may obtain mercy,
and find grace to help in time of need."*

Hebrews 4:16

Have you ever gotten an unexpected phone call relaying some bad news? Probably so. But listen. When we call on Dr. Jesus—the GREAT PHYSICIAN, the bad news can be turned into glad news! Maybe you need some glad news today.

The following is a true story. One day, a few years ago, while carrying out the many pastoral duties, my phone rang. It was obvious this Christian man was very distraught. With a quivering voice, he explained that numerous scans had revealed that his wife had a brain tumor. I questioned him about the diagnosis and he confirmed that numerous tests and scans had been done, and by a credible doctor.

After hearing this dreadful news, his wife—Debbie, requested prayer. That very night we gathered at her house and circled around her. We lifted up her physical needs to our Father's *"throne of grace"*— putting it in His hands.

Not long after, early before sun up one morning, we made our way to Emory Hospital in Atlanta, Georgia. Debbie was scheduled for extensive surgery to remove the tumor. When we arrived at the hospital, we proceeded downstairs to see her as she awaited surgery. The doctors had already installed the HALLO to her forehead (a metal ring attached by screws). After praying with her once again, we made our way upstairs where other family members were anxiously waiting.

Several hours had passed when her doctor finally entered the room. He had a very puzzled look on his face as he began to share, "We drilled down through her skull only to discover there was NOTHING there! NO TUMOR!! NO MASS!!!" He couldn't explain it! He really didn't have to, for in our minds—our Lord had healed her.

Needless to say, we all began to shout and rejoice over this answer to prayer. Our Lord—Jehovah Jireh, had touched her body. As far as the family was concerned—it was a supernatural miracle! The mighty hand of the GREAT PHYSICIAN had healed her body.

What a mighty God we serve! Jesus Christ gets the glory.

Is it God's will to heal everyone all the time? Is it a lack of faith if someone is not healed after being prayed over? While our Lord does heal our bodies in answer to prayer according to His purpose and plan, it obviously is not His will to heal all. If that were the case, then no one would ever die, or get sick. And yet at the same time—it is our responsibility as believers to ask and pray according to His will.

PRAYER POWER

"More things are wrought by prayer than this world dreams," are the words of Alfred Tennyson, the most renowned poet of the nineteenth century. It has been said Queen Mary of Scots feared the prayers of John Knox more than any army of 10,000 men! Matthew Henry, beloved minister and prolific writer, made the statement, "When God is up to a work, He puts His people to praying." Thomas Watson, the Puritan preacher, said, "The tree of promise will not drop its fruit, unless shaken by the hand of prayer."

What breathing is to the lung—prayer is to the Christian. Prayer is communion with God. It is both talking and listening to Him. The main purpose of prayer is to glorify God. Sad to say, many people only use prayer, just when they feel it's needed. Nonetheless, in the Word of God—the believer hears the need to pray, reads the great prayer promises, observes the prayer provisions, and witnesses the power of prayer. The Word of God stands—and we can stand on it!

PRAYER PLEAS

Jesus Christ—the One who instituted prayer, extends an invitation to all believers to draw near to His throne, because it is a *"throne of grace."*

> *Seeing then that we have a great high priest, that is passed into the heavens, Jesus the Son of God, let us hold fast our profession. For we have not an high priest which cannot be touched with the feeling of our infirmities; but was in all points tempted like as we are, yet without sin. Let us therefore come boldly unto the throne of grace, that we may obtain mercy, and find grace to help in time of need* (Heb. 4:14-16).

This is definitely an urgent plea. *"Let us therefore come."* The place is *"the throne of grace."* The believer is to come *"boldly."*

First, the great place is a *"throne of grace."* In Old Testament times, it was the mercy seat. Only the high priest could enter into the Holy of Holies and sprinkle the blood of a goat as an atonement, or covering, for the sins of the people. This was done once a year on September the 25th (Lev. 16) and was called the Day of Atonement, or Yom Kippur. However, when Jesus Christ—*the lamb that taketh away the sins of the world* (John 1-29)—said, *"It is finished,"* the veil that separated sinful humanity from a holy God (with the exception of the High Priest), was rent from top to bottom; thereby giving every born-again believer access into the everlasting covenant (Heb. 10-19).

Second, this passage teaches that Jesus extends a warm invitation to come. Somebody asks why? The answer is… because He is the problem solver. He knows all things. He cares about the believer. *"Humble yourselves therefore under the mighty hand of God, that he may exalt you in due time: Casting all your care upon him; for he careth for you"* (1 Pet. 5:6-7).

Yet—how is the believer to approach the throne of grace? The Bible says *"boldly."* The word "boldly" signifies without restraint or with liberty. Boldly could be translated "all speech," meaning holding nothing back. This of course does not mean proudly or defiantly, but rather humbly.

What are some reasons for the believer to approach the throne? Because we need mercy constantly and grace daily. Thank God, we don't need justice, but rather mercy and grace. It is like the woman who had her picture taken and did not like the photograph at all. She called up the photographer, "This picture you took did not do me justice!" He responded, "Ma'am, you don't need justice, you need mercy!"

PRAYER PROMISES

God's Word is full of wonderful prayer promises. Listen to the words of Jesus, *"If ye being evil, know how to give good gifts unto your children, how much more shall your father which is in heaven give good things to them that ask him?"* (Matt. 7:11). This of course, was after He said to ask and keep on asking, to seek and keep on seeking, and to knock persistently (Matt. 7:7).

Reading and memorizing the prayer promises of God builds faith and confidence (Rom. 10:17). For example, Ephesians 3:20 says, *"Now unto him that is able to do exceeding abundantly above all that we ask or think, according to the power that worketh in us."* The Apostle John writes in 1 John 5:14-15,

> *This is the confidence that we have in him, that if we ask anything according to His will, he heareth us: and if we know that he hears us whatsoever we ask, we know that we have the petitions that we desired of him.*

Jeremiah 33:3 states, *"Call unto me, and I will answer thee and show thee great and mighty things, which thou knowest not."* Aren't you glad when you call heaven, you don't get an answering machine? "Press 1 to speak to Mary. Press 2 for Peter." I don't want to talk with Mary or Peter—I want to talk with Jesus! Why? He made us! He loves us! He died for us! He knows us! He arose for us... and He's coming back for us!

Consider the following prayer promises:

- Psalm 34:15—*The eyes of the Lord are upon the righteous, and his ears are open unto their cry.*
- Psalm 50:15—*And call upon me in the day of trouble: I will deliver thee, and thou shalt glorify me.*

- 2 Chronicles 7:14—*If my people, which are called by my name, shall humble themselves, and pray, and seek my face, and turn from their wicked ways; then will I hear from heaven, and will forgive their sin, and will heal their land.*

- Isaiah 55:6—*Seek ye the Lord while he may be found, call ye upon him while he is near:*

- Matthew 18:19-20—*Again I say unto you, that if two of you shall agree on earth as touching any thing that they shall ask, it shall be done for them of my Father which is in heaven. For where two or three are gathered together in my name, there am I in the midst of them.*

- Luke 18:6-8— *And the Lord said, Hear what the unjust judge saith. And shall not God avenge his own elect, which cry day and night unto him, though he bear long with them? I tell you that he will avenge them speedily. Nevertheless when the Son of man cometh, shall he find faith on the earth?*

- John 14:13-14—*And whatsoever ye shall ask in my name, that will I do, that the Father may be glorified in the Son. If ye shall ask any thing in my name, I will do it.*

- John 15:7—*If ye abide in me, and my words abide in you, ye shall ask what ye will, and it shall be done unto you.*

- John 16:24—*Hitherto have ye asked nothing in my name: ask, and ye shall receive, that your joy may be full.*

- Philippians 4:6-7—*Be careful for nothing; but in every thing by prayer and supplication with thanksgiving let your requests be made known unto God. And the peace of God, which passeth all understanding, shall keep your hearts and minds through Christ Jesus.*

- James 1:5—*If any of you lack wisdom, let him ask of God, that giveth to all men liberally, and upbraideth not; and it shall be given him.*

- James 4:2—*Ye lust, and have not: ye kill, and desire to have, and cannot obtain: ye fight and war, yet ye have not, because ye ask not.*

- James 5:16—*Confess your faults one to another, and pray one for another, that ye may be healed. The effectual fervent prayer of a righteous man availeth much.*

The disciples said, *"Lord teach us to pray"* (Luke 11:1). Jesus said, *"Men ought always to pray, and not to faint"* (Luke 18:1). The word "faint" means lose heart. The truth of the matter is that all Christians need to be enrolled in Christ's School of Prayer. One never graduates from this school!

Have you gotten discouraged? Are your prayers delayed? Why? God's timing? My preaching professor—the late Dr. Stephen Olford, used to say in his British accent, "Pray when you feel like it. Pray when you don't feel like it. Pray until you feel like it!"

PRAYER PROVISIONS

In the Word of God, there are also wonderful provisions concerning prayer. The first provision is the Son of God who intercedes for the saints (Heb. 7:25). *"Who is he that condemneth? It is Christ that died, yea rather, that is risen again, who is even at the right hand of God, who also maketh intercession for us"* (Rom. 8:34). *"Wherefore he is able also to save them to the uttermost that come unto God by him, seeing he ever liveth to make intercession for them"* (Heb. 7:25). Remember, Jesus prayed for Peter. *"And the Lord said, Simon, Simon, behold, Satan hath desired to have you, that he may sift you as wheat:"* (Luke 22:31). It is so encouraging to know He can sympathize with our weaknesses (Heb. 4:15). He is our advocate who ever pleads our case before the Father.

> *My little children, these things write I unto you, that ye sin not. And if any man sin, we have an advocate with the Father, Jesus Christ the righteous* (1 John 2:1).

The next prayer provision is God the Holy Spirit. The Bible says the Holy Spirit makes intercession through the saints according to the will of God.

> *Likewise the Spirit also helpeth our infirmities: for we know not what we should pray for as we ought: but the Spirit itself maketh intercession for us with groanings which cannot be uttered. And he that searcheth the hearts knoweth what is the mind of the Spirit, because he maketh intercession for the saints according to the will of God* (Rom. 8:26-27).

Spurgeon, the "Prince of Preachers," said in regards to this verse, that it is much like a child coming to his or her parents so excited about something that the parent has to help the child express his or her thoughts by speaking for them.[1] This is true with the third person of the Trinity.

Prayer is a cycle involving the Trinity—the Father births the prayers, the Son intercedes on behalf of the saints, and the Holy Spirit, because of our infirmities, makes intercession for us *"with groanings which cannot be uttered"* because He searches our heart (Rom. 8:26-27). Each believer has the awesome privilege of praying or interceding for men and women, and boys and girls on earth. Who can explain the Trinity? A little boy came very close when he said, "The Trinity is three in one and one in three and the one in the middle died for me!" That's pretty good theology!

PRAYER PRINCIPLES

What are the basic principles of prayer? How should one pray? A Christian should pray reverently like Solomon (2 Chron. 6:13). He knelt down.

> *For Solomon had made a brasen scaffold of five cubits long, and five cubits broad, and three cubits high, and had set it in the midst of the court: and upon it he stood, and kneeled down upon his knees before all the congregation of Israel, and spread forth his hands toward heaven.*

When Moses, Aaron, and Joshua had an encounter with the living God, they fell on their faces (Num. 20-26; Jos. 5:14). Elijah put his face between his knees when he prayed (1 Kings 18:42). King Jehoshaphat bowed his head and placed his face on the ground (2 Chron. 20:18). Jesus Christ fell on His face (Matt. 26:39). Tradition says James was called "camel knees."

A Christian should pray continually like Daniel.

> *Now when Daniel knew that the writing was signed, he went into his house; and his windows being open in his chamber toward Jerusalem, he kneeled upon his knees three times a day, and prayed, and gave thanks before his God, as he did aforetime* (Dan. 6:10).

He prayed at least three times a day.

A Christian should pray worshipfully—"*O come, let us worship and bow down: let us kneel before the Lord our maker*" (Psa. 95:6), secretly— "*But thou, when thou prayest, enter into thy closet, and when thou hast shut thy door, pray to thy Father which is in secret; and thy Father which seeth in secret shall reward thee openly"* (Matt. 6:6), and unceasingly—*"Pray without ceasing"* (1 Thess. 5:17).

He or she should pray forgivingly,

> *And they stoned Stephen, calling upon God, and saying, Lord Jesus, receive my spirit, And he kneeled down, and cried with a loud voice, Lord, lay not this sin to their charge. And when he had said this, he fell asleep* (Acts 7:59-60).

and as Jesus did, submissively—*"And he was withdrawn from them about a stone's cast, and kneeled down, and prayed, Saying, Father, if thou be willing, remove this cup from me: nevertheless not my will, but thine, be done."* (Luke 22:41-42). A well-balanced prayer includes adoration—or worship, and supplication—or telling God your needs.

> *Be careful for nothing; but in every thing by prayer and supplication with thanksgiving let your requests be made known unto God. And the peace of God, which passeth all understanding, shall keep your hearts and minds through Christ Jesus* (Phil. 4:6-7).

A Christian should offer prayer in Jesus' name. *"And whatsoever ye shall ask in my name, that will I do, that the Father may be glorified in the Son. If ye shall ask any thing in my name, I will do it"* (John 14:1-14).

Finally, a Christian should pray in FAITH. God gives a measure of faith (Rom. 12:3). The Lord Jesus Christ spoke about prayer and faith.

> *And Jesus answering saith unto them, Have faith in God. For verily I say unto you, That whosoever shall say unto this mountain, Be thou removed, and be thou cast into the*

> *sea; and shall not doubt in his heart, but shall believe that those things which he saith shall come to pass; he shall have whatsoever he saith. Therefore I say unto you, What things soever ye desire, when ye pray, believe that ye receive them, and ye shall have them* (Mark 11:22-24).

The prayer of faith *recognizes* the will of God, *rests* on the promise of Christ, *relies* on the power of God, *responds* to the Spirit of God, and finally, *rejoices* in the answer from God.

PRAYER PATTERNS

The Lord Jesus gave His twelve disciples, yea all His disciples, a model prayer which is found in the sixth chapter of the book of Matthew (v. 9-13).

> *After this manner therefore pray ye: Our Father which art in heaven, Hallowed be thy name. Thy kingdom come, Thy will be done in earth, as it is in heaven. Give us this day our daily bread. And forgive us our debts, as we forgive our debtors. And lead us not into temptation, but deliver us from evil: For thine is the kingdom, and the power, and the glory, for ever. Amen.*

Jesus' High Priestly Prayer is recorded in John 17. Spurgeon referred to this prayer as the "Golden Prayer."[2] In this Farewell Prayer, Jesus prayed for Himself, His disciples, and all believers. The life of Christ was saturated with prayer. In fact, one could easily say it was a life of prayer. Jesus prayed early in the morning—*"And in the morning, rising up a great while before day, he went out, and departed into a solitary place, and there prayed"* (Mark 1:35). Jesus prayed in the evening.

> *And when he had sent them away, he departed into a mountain to pray. And when even was come, the ship was in the midst of the sea, and he alone on the land* (Mark 6:46-47).

Jesus prayed alone—*"And he withdrew himself into the wilderness, and prayed"* (Luke 5:16), and He prayed with His disciples—*"And it came to pass in those days, that he went out into a mountain to pray, and continued all night in prayer to God"* (Luke 6:12).

Furthermore, Jesus agonized in prayer (Heb. 5:7; Luke 22). He agreed in prayer to the Father's will—*"not my will."*

> *And he was withdrawn from them about a stone's cast, and kneeled down, and prayed, Saying, Father, if thou be willing, remove this cup from me: nevertheless not my will, but thine, be done. And there appeared an angel unto him from heaven, strengthening him. And being in an agony he prayed more earnestly: and his sweat was as it were great drops of blood falling down to the ground* (Luke 22:41-44).

He taught the importance of unity in prayer.

> *Again I say unto you, that if two of you shall agree on earth as touching any thing that they shall ask, it shall be done for them of my Father which is in heaven. For where two or three are gathered together in my name, there am I in the midst of them* (Matt. 18:19-20).

Jesus was anointed with power as He preached and prayed.

> *And there was delivered unto him the book of the prophet*

Esaias. And when he had opened the book, he found the place where it was written, The Spirit of the Lord is upon me, because he hath anointed me to preach the gospel to the poor; he hath sent me to heal the brokenhearted, to preach deliverance to the captives, and recovering of sight to the blind, to set at liberty them that are bruised (Luke 4:17-18).

Jesus lived a life of prayer and demonstrated for His followers—great prayer patterns. Will you follow the prayer patterns that Jesus left, which include a life of dedication and discipline? If so, then every believer can experience the joys of a prayer life that profits!

PRAYER PROFITS

Prayer is profitable! Consider the following: It was through the power of prayer that Abraham's servant Eliezar found a wife for Isaac. Prayer was the tool that changed Abram's name to Abraham, and Jacob's name to Israel. Prayer was the channel that brought the plagues to Egypt, parted the Red Sea, turned the bitter water of Marah to sweet water, and caused manna to be rained down from heaven.

It was through the power of prayer that Israel was victorious over Amalek, and the children of Israel were healed in the midst of the fiery serpents. Prayer was the instrument that uncovered Achan's sin and stayed or held still the sun and the moon for Joshua to defeat the Amorites. Gideon was encouraged and strengthened to break down the altar of Baal and cut down the Asherah pole thru prayer. He also witnessed the Midianites running for their life because of the power of God! Samson was endued with power one last time as he prayed. Hannah's prayers were answered as she conceived a son named Samuel. Solomon received great wisdom due to prayer.

The Prophet Elijah prayed and life was restored to the widow's son. He again prayed and God shut up the windows of heaven so that it did not rain three and a half years. He then entreated the Lord and God sent the rain! Still further, it was Elijah, who prayed and saw the fire fall and consume the sacrifice on top of Mt. Carmel.

King Hezekiah saw the hand of God move as a result of prayer. He was told to put his house in order for his time had come. Consequently, he cried out to the Lord. God added fifteen years to his life, confirming it by turning the shadow dial back ten degrees.

Nehemiah was encouraged and empowered when he prayed. Despite the opposition, he rebuilt the walls in fifty-two days. It was through the power of prayer that Daniel interpreted King Nebuchadnezzar's dream. Moreover, God delivered Daniel from the lion's den, and Jonah from the belly of the great fish. He delivered Peter from within the midst of the jail as the Church prayed.

Finally, the great outpouring of the Holy Spirit happened when one hundred and twenty believers assembled together in unity and cried out to Almighty God. Prayer is unquestionably powerful and profitable! So why are so many Christians and churches powerless? *"Ye have not because ye ask not"* (Jas. 4:2).

Pray brother! Pray sister!!

CHAPTER TWO
THE PURPOSE OF PRAYER

*"And they continued steadfastly
in the apostles' doctrine and fellowship,
and in breaking of bread, and in prayer."*

Acts 2:42

The year was 1996. The place was New Rocky Creek Baptist Church. The purpose was A CALL for one day a week of PRAYER and FASTING for revival in America and in the Church.

Starting the first Saturday in January of that year and going all year long every Saturday from 1:00 p.m. until sometimes midnight, the church doors were opened for intercession. Our Lord put it in our hearts to CALL a solemn ASSEMBLY for crying out to Him for His blessings!

Following the pattern of Joel the prophet, the church, along with pastors from out of town, gathered to seek the Lord. Needless to say, it was well worth spending the time in His PRESENCE, getting filled up with His POWER and worshiping the person of Jesus Christ.

Interestingly enough, when we pray for certain things the Spirit of God begins to transform our will into our Father's will. Admittedly, there were numerous days when the load of the prayer meeting was carried by only a few Christians. But after all—Jesus did say,

> *Again I say unto you, That if two of you shall agree on earth as touching any thing that they shall ask, it shall be done for them of my Father which is in heaven. For where two or three are gathered together in my name, there am I in the midst of them* (Matt. 18:19-20).

It doesn't take 100! Jesus only had twelve disciples, really eleven; and He did say—if just two. The prayer lesson is UNITY and PERSEVERANCE. *"And when they had prayed, the place was shaken where they were assembled together; and they were all filled with the Holy Ghost, and they spake the word of God with boldness"* (Acts 4:31). There is power in prayer when we agree together according to the will of God.

What did our Lord do in answer to prayer during those special days? From a tangible point of view, at least three men were called out as pastors to preach the gospel. All three of those men are still serving as pastors even today. A man who was a teenager at the time was recently ordained into the gospel ministry and is now serving in a local church. Praise the Lord!

Gifted Sunday School teachers were called out who are still serving at New Rocky Creek today. Several godly deacons were raised up who are still faithfully serving our Lord. We experienced exponential GROWTH through the Sunday School—the average attendance went from in the fifties to over one hundred in just a couple of years.

In addition—while experiencing growing pains, a team of men in the church began to meet and pray with gifted leaders in the church to prepare plans for building a nine thousand square foot multipurpose building. It was completed a couple of years later through the hard work of men and women along with volunteers from other churches.

Our Lord was doing a MIGHTY work among us! *"Behold ye among the heathen, and regard, and wonder marvellously: for I will work a work in your days, which ye will not believe, though it be told you"* (Hab. 1:5).

Even until this day, the BLESSINGS of the Lord continue to fall upon New Rocky Creek with a great staff, faithful deacons, and a strong Sunday School. It has been life's highest privilege to serve Jesus Christ through New Rocky Creek Baptist Church these last thirty-two years.

Hudson Taylor—the great missionary to China, once said, "God's work, done God's way, in God's timing, with God's power, gets God's blessing." The Church moves forward on her knees! If the early church in the book of Acts is a pattern to follow, it is crystal clear that praying in faith is one of the main ingredients to church growth (Acts 1:14, 2:42, 4:24-31, etc.). The early church literally exploded like a blaze of light streaking across the midnight sky. The devil could not stop it. The world could not choke it. God's truth marched forward. *"And the Lord added to the church daily such as should be saved"* (Acts 2:47).

What does praying in faith have to do with church growth? Our Great Shepherd is ready, willing, and able to release heaven's power upon His sheep. He knows where to find the green pastures and the still waters. Jesus died for the Church (Acts 20:28); thus, He purchased it with His own blood. Furthermore, the Bridegroom is coming back soon to receive His lovely bride (Eph. 5:25f; 1 Thess. 4:16-17).

The problem today unfortunately, is that man is trying to build his own church. Jesus did not say, I will build your church. Neither did He say—you will build my church. Rather, He said, *"I will build my church…"* (Matt. 16:18). Pastors and people need to stand on His promises like Abraham of old.

> *(As it is written, I have made thee a father of many nations,) before him whom he believed, even God, who*

> *quickeneth the dead, and calleth those things which be not as though they were. Who against hope believed in hope, that he might become the father of many nations, according to that which was spoken, So shall thy seed be. And being not weak in faith, he considered not his own body now dead, when he was about an hundred years old, neither yet the deadness of Sarah's womb: He staggered not at the promise of God through unbelief; but was strong in faith, giving glory to God; And being fully persuaded that, what he had promised, he was able also to perform* (Rom. 4:17-21).

As co-laborers, we need to cooperate with the Head of the Body—Jesus Christ (Eph. 1:21-22). When the Church needs money for the ministry, He owns the cattle on a thousand hills—and the hill! He knows where the money's at in the fishes mouth! When the Church needs spiritual leaders, Jesus said, *"Pray ye therefore the Lord of the harvest, that he will send forth laborers into his harvest;"* (Matt. 9:38). When the pastor and people need wisdom, James under the inspiration of the Holy Spirit says—just ask (Jas. 1:5). When long-range plans are needed, the prophet Jeremiah says—just call upon the Lord, who will answer and show you great and mighty things (Jer. 33:3).

How does the Lord grow His Church through praying in faith? Here are seven ways: (1) it *necessitates* relationships, (2) it *initiates* needed changes, (3) it *activates* evangelism, (4) it *stimulates* spirit-anointing preaching and teaching, (5) it *permeates* leadership, (6) it *dictates* God's activity in the Church, and (7) it *agitates* the release of power.

First of all, praying in faith *necessitates* relationships. *"Can two walk together, except they be agreed,"* (Amos 3:3). Another glance at the vibrant, dynamic, spirit-filled early church reveals secrets to meaningful relationships. *"And they continued steadfastly in the apostles' doctrine and fellowship, and in breaking of bread, and in prayer,"* (Acts 2:42). Through prayer, hearts are made pure. Through prayer, hearts are knitted together—that is where real bonding takes place. Through prayer, consciences become clear. Through prayer, the love of God is poured out into waiting, trusting, and thirsty hearts (Rom. 5:5). This overflows and runs out like a river into other's lives. Love becomes an unbreakable bond that builds lasting relationships—love for Jesus, love for others (1 Cor. 13:1f; 1 John 3:14, 13:35; Eph. 4:2-3; Phil. 2:1-4).

Of course, the main purpose of praying in faith is to glorify the Lord. *"When a man's ways please the Lord, he maketh even his enemies to be at peace with him,"* (Prov. 16:7). If talking to the Father about each other and then obeying His counsel does not build relationships—they will never be built.

Second, the prayer of faith *initiates* needed changes. God knows how to remove old mountains of tradition that block His Church from growing.

> *For verily I say unto you, that whosoever shall say unto this mountain, be thou, and be thou cast into the sea; and shall not doubt in his heart, but shall believe that those things which he saith shall come to pass; he shall have what so ever he saith. Therefore I say unto you, what things soever ye desire, when ye pray, believe that ye receive them, and ye shall have them* (Mark 11:23-24).

Thank God, the Lord still moves stones from the tomb of, "We've always done it this way." When the Master calls forth His bride as He did Lazarus, she will rise from the slumbering grave! The Lord of Glory can take a backslidden church (Ephesus), a worldly church (Pergamos), a feminine church (Thyatira), a dead church (Sardis), and a lukewarm church (Laodicea), and make them all into a loving, praying, soul winning church like Philadelphia.

Changes take place when God's people pray in faith because it releases God's power which paralyzes the enemy and tears down strongholds (2 Cor. 10:3-5; Eph. 6:10-18). As long as the enemy has jurisdiction to operate from, he will come and go as he pleases. That is why the devil fights the effectual fervent prayer (literally boiling over) of a righteous man more than anything else. The Greek reads that this kind of praying has "great strength." No wonder the plans of Haman were frustrated when Esther called her people to fast and pray for three days. No wonder Queen Mary of Scots feared the prayers of John Knox more than the army of 10,000 men.

When God's servant and His people begin to pray in faith—changes take place because God's vision is revealed. *"Where there is no vision, the people perish: but he that keepeth the law, happy is he"* (Prov. 29:18). Once His vision is known, the Lord's guidance is sought through prayer as to how to fulfill the vision. Unfortunately, this is where some churches crash! There is always the danger of going ahead of God without His glorious presence (Exod. 33:1f). On the other hand, there is the temptation to lag behind until everything is figured out humanly speaking. This tragedy results in leaning on the arm of flesh through human reasoning rather than trusting and walking by faith (Rom. 1:17; Zech. 4:5-6; Jer. 17:5). This dishonors the Lord and consequently—His Spirit is grieved. Church growth is stunted.

Not only does praying in faith enhance relationships and create changes, but third, it *activates* evangelism. Billy Graham, the great evangelist, once said, the key to evangelism is threefold: prayer, prayer, and prayer. Bible scholar and evangelist, R.A. Torrey, states in his article, *The Place of Prayer in Evangelism*, "The most important human factor in effective evangelism is prayer." He cites passages in the Book of Acts that resulted from the ten-day prayer meeting (Acts 1:4). *"There were added unto them in that day about 3,000 souls,"* (Acts 2:41-47). He then traces every great awakening from the Book of Acts until our modern day, declaring that all of them had their earthly origin in prayer. For example, the great awakening in the 18th century began with Jonathan Edward's famous "call to prayer." David Brainerd's work among the North American Indians was bathed in prayer day and night before God. Charles Finney was God's instrument of revival in 1830. In Rochester, New York, there were reports that about 100,000 persons were connected with churches because of God's mighty power—speaking of church growth!

Prayer was the spark that ignited a move of God's Spirit in 1857, across America, known as the Fulton Street prayer meeting. Thousands were converted to the Church. The flame of prayer burned brightly again in 1873, under D.L. Moody, and again in 1904 and 1905, in the great Welsh revival. Over 100,000 precious souls were born again. Like a tidal wave, revival swept across Africa, India, China, Korea, and America. In Paducah, Kentucky, the First Baptist Church reported adding over one thousand new converts to its roll. The pastor reportedly died from exhaustion. Historians estimate somewhere close to twenty million people accepted Jesus Christ as their Lord and Savior while this revival inferno burned in America. Wow! Do it again Lord!

Torrey said that we are placing more and more dependence upon men, machinery, methods, and less and less upon God. What is needed today, Torrey declared, above all else—is prayer, true prayer in the power of the Holy Ghost. Lord, teach us to pray!

Fourth, praying in faith *stimulates* spirit-anointed preaching and teaching. In the *Criswell Guidebook for Pastors*, W.A. Criswell writes that successful pastors of growing churches like Stephen Olford, Charles Spurgeon, and Charles Stanley affirmed that the power to preach comes from God's throne room.[1] The great prayer warrior and pastor,

E.M. Bounds, in his writings on prayer states, "Prayer makes preaching strong, gives it unction, and makes it stick. A prayerless preacher is a misnomer. He has either missed his calling, or has grievously failed God who called him into the ministry."[2] John Wesley was right when he said, "If your sermon does not have fire in it, throw it in the fire!"

Speaking of prayer in the life and ministry of pastors, Peter Wagner in his book *Prayer Shield*, entitles a chapter "Secret of Pastors' Prayer Lives." In this chapter, he records the results of his personal survey of 572 American pastors and the actual time each spent in prayer a day. This is what he discovered:[3]

> 57% prayed less than 30 minutes,
> 34% prayed 20 minutes to one hour, and
> 9% prayed one hour or more.

The average prayer time was 22 minutes daily.

In his study, he compared American pastors' prayer time with that of pastors in other countries. He recorded the following:

> Australia – 23 minutes a day,
> New Zealand – 30 minutes a day,
> Japan – 44 minutes a day, and
> Korea – 90 minutes a day.

Bottom line—prayer works if you work it!

"*Ye have not, because ye ask not,*" (Jas. 4:2).

"*And when they prayed, the place was shaken… and they were all filled with the Holy Ghost, and they spake the word of God with boldness*" (Acts 4:31).

Fifth, praying in faith *permeates* leadership. More work should mean more prayer according to Martin Luther. He said, "Work, work from early till late. In fact, I have so much to do that I shall spend the first three hours in prayer." Look at the greatest leader of all time, Jesus. His life was saturated with prayer—in the morning (Mark 1:35), in the evening, all night (Mark 6:46-47), alone (Luke 5:16), and with His disciples (Luke 6:12). Look at the lives of God's great leaders such as Moses, Nehemiah, David, Paul, and the Pastor of Jerusalem who was called "camel knees"—James. These were men of prayer. Since leadership is the ability to move and influence people, Hudson Taylor was right when he said, "It is possible to move men, through God, by prayer alone."

> Prayer moves the arm
> that moves the world
> to bring deliverance down.

Author unknown.

Sixth, prevailing prayer or praying in faith—*dictates* God's activity in the Church, and seventh, praying in faith—*agitates* the release of His mighty power. E.M. Bounds stated, "Praying men keep God in the church in full force."[4] To put it another way, as Pastor C.H. Spurgeon used to say, "the battles are fought and won on our knees."

When God's people pray in faith, the heavens are opened. The fire falls! Torrential blessings rain down and water thirsty lands. The breath of heaven moves. Mighty rushing winds refresh weary souls. The shekinah glory hovers over God's Church. Hurting Christians and hell-bound sinners are ushered in to encounter a living, Holy God! Healing takes place. The cries of newborn babes are heard. Families are reconciled. People are restored. God is glorified! Hallelujah! *"Unto him be glory in the church"!* (Eph. 3:21).

CHAPTER THREE

THE POWER OF PRAYER AND FASTING

"Is not this the fast that I have chosen?
to loose the bands of wickedness,
to undo the heavy burdens,
and to let the oppressed go free,
and that ye break every yoke?"

Isaiah 58:6

God still calls His people to times of prayer and fasting (Joel 2:15-17). When done with the right motives, praying and fasting not only brings personal revival but also stirs the heart of the believer for the salvation of the lost (Isa. 58:1-14; Matt. 6:16-18). In his book *Fasting for Spiritual Breakthrough*, Elmer Towns wrote,

> In the early eighteenth century, the great evangelist Jonathan Edwards fasted for 24 hours before preaching the sermon many claim sparked the revival in New England that grew in to the First Awakening. The sermon was called "Sinners in the Hands of an Angry God."[1]

Speaking on the same subject, Bill Bright shared these words about the Welsh revival.

> Men prayer brigades began to form. These men would

pray into the night—sometimes all night—for God to rouse other men out of bed, convict them of sin, and save their souls. There were reports of men crawling out of bed in the middle of the night, finding a meeting and crying out to the Lord Jesus to save them.[2]

History has proven the power of prayer and fasting. Lord send a revival, and let it begin in me! Jesus not only taught fasting (Matt. 6:16-18), but He also demonstrated it.

And Jesus being full of the Holy Ghost returned from Jordan, and was led by the Spirit into the wilderness, Being forty days tempted of the devil. And in those days he did eat nothing: and when they were ended, he afterward hungered (Luke 4:1-2).

Jesus was full of the Holy Spirit and power, yet He still fasted forty days and nights. Interestingly, He first had to overcome Satan's temptations before entering into His public ministry.

Secondly, Paul fasted three days after his conversion in preparation for his evangelistic ministry. *"And he was three days without sight, and neither did eat nor drink"* (Acts 9:9). In fact, before Paul and Barnabas were sent out of Antioch into the mission field, the leaders fasted and prayed. *"And when they had fasted and prayed, and laid their hands on them, they sent..."* (Acts 13:3). Derek Prince wrote, "They still required the impartation of the special grace and power that were needed for the task that lay ahead."[3] Furthermore, Paul and Barnabas ordained elders in the churches. They *"prayed with fasting"* (Acts 14:23). Prayer is God's atomic bomb, but prayer and fasting is God's nuclear bomb!!

Shortly after receiving Jesus Christ as my personal Lord and Savior, I was introduced to the purpose, principles, and power of fasting. Immediately, through prayer and seeking our Lord—the great benefits of fasting were revealed to me. During the first week of a total fast (just water), I learned several lifelong lessons. Over the last four decades, it has been a great privilege to experience many breakthroughs because of the power of prayer and fasting. Here are a few helpful hints.

1. Spend time in prayer when fasting by drawing near to the God of the Bible—He makes it well worth our minor sacrifices.

2. When your facing spiritual battles that cannot be overcome any other way, purpose in your heart to cry out to God through fasting—He will respond in His timing.

3. Understand—fasting is not a manipulating game; i.e., "If I do this Lord, then I expect you to do this." Instead, one of the main purposes for fasting is to enjoy fellowship and intimacy with Jesus.

4. Be ready to see how much of the flesh is in control of your life when depriving the cravings of our flesh—yet get ready for spiritual growth to take place.

5. Get ready to see spiritual truth in a different light.

6. The motives of people will become clearer as we fast with the right motives.

7. Expect to be broken—the flesh is weak, but the spirit willing.

8. Be aware that others will not understand.

9. Please do not fast as a diet, unless that is what you are doing—dieting.

10. Do not over-gorge on food when breaking your fast, but slowly allow your stomach to get adjusted.

11. Stay focused on what the Holy Spirit is doing in your life.

12. Be careful not to be boastful—sometimes because of pride we feel superior because we are fasting.

13. Be led by the Spirit as to the length of the fast (fasting is probably not a good idea at Thanksgiving).

14. Don't rob God of glory—but be sure to give Him the Glory!

Do you need a breakthrough? To God be the glory… our Lord Jesus has led us, through His Church—New Rocky Creek Baptist, to have numerous extended forty-day fasts, twenty-one-day fasts, three-day fasts, etc. Jesus practiced fasting. If it was good for Him—it is good for me!

Jesus said, *"when you fast,"* not—if you fast (Matt. 6:16). *"When you fast"*—be blessed and be a blessing!

CHAPTER FOUR
THE PRACTICE OF PRAYER: DAILY DEVOTIONALS

*"And it came to pass, that,
as he was praying in a certain place,
when he ceased, one of his disciples said unto him,
Lord, teach us to pray..."*

Luke 11:1

This chapter includes daily devotionals covering the whole spectrum of the practice of prayer, from praying with the right motives, to engaging the enemy—interceding for others, to fasting and praying for spiritual breakthrough. The disciples asked Jesus, *"...Lord teach us to pray..."* (Luke 11:1). Careful study of this chapter will help every Christian be better equipped to pray and to begin experiencing the rewards of a powerful prayer life.

These daily devotionals will be especially purposeful for preachers, teachers, missionaries—or anyone who has been called to teach the Word of God through exegetical, historical, grammatical, doctrinal, and practical perspectives.

PRAYER WORKS IF YOU WORK IT

Introduction: Do you believe... "PRAYER WORKS"? It really

does, if you work it! Are you working it? If not, will you start—to see it works... if you work it?

The prophet Daniel is writing during the 70-year captivity of the Jews in Babylon, prophesied by Jeremiah (Jer. 25:10-11). Because of their negligence in allowing the land to lay rest as God instructed them in Leviticus 25, the southern kingdom of Judah was hauled away by Nebuchadnezzar and his armies. Meanwhile, the Lord had plans for them to return after the allotted time of 70 years (for each year they failed to obey the Lord). A study in the book of Daniel reveals four key ingredients that come together to make "PRAYER WORK."

1. How does God "WORK thru the POWER of PRAYER"?

> *Then Daniel went in, and desired of the king that he would give him time, and that he would shew the king the interpretation* (Dan. 2:16).

> *I thank thee, and praise thee, O thou God of my fathers, who hast given me wisdom and might, and hast made known unto me now what we desired of thee: for thou hast now made known unto us the king's matter* (Dan. 2:23).

God reveals things, *"In His Time"* (v. 16). He does this, *"All for His Glory"* (v. 23). In Daniel's case, the Lord revealed the meaning of the king's dream through prayer. Likewise, the Holy Spirit reveals insights as we pray in faith.

2. When does God "WORK thru the POWER of PRAYER"?

> *Then Daniel went to his house, and made the thing known to Hananiah, Mishael, and Azariah, his companions* (Dan. 2:17).

There are two important factors to "When does God 'WORK thru the POWER of PRAYER'":

- When there is unity (v. 17).
- When there is maturity (v. 17).

Will you get someone to agree in faith with you?

3. What does God "WORK thru the POWER of PRAYER"?

> *And the decree went forth that the wise men should be slain; and they sought Daniel and his fellows to be slain* (Dan. 2:13).

> *That they would desire mercies of the God of heaven concerning this secret; that Daniel and his fellows should not perish with the rest of the wise men of Babylon* (Dan. 2:18).

The Lord realigns our "will"—not wheel (v. 18).

4. Where does God "WORK in answer to the POWER of PRAYER"?

> *Daniel answered and said, Blessed be the name of God for ever and ever: for wisdom and might are his: And he changeth the times and the seasons: he removeth kings, and setteth up kings: he giveth wisdom unto the wise, and knowledge to them that know understanding: He revealeth the deep and secret things: he knoweth what is in the darkness, and the light dwelleth with him. I thank thee, and praise thee, O thou God of my fathers, who hast given me wisdom and might, and hast made known unto me now what we desired of thee: for thou hast now made known unto us the king's matter* (Dan. 2:20-23).

When the Lord Jesus answers prayer we ought to THANK Him. Like Daniel, we are to acknowledge Him as Creator of all things—including seasons.

Conclusion: Since our Lord sets up kings and removes them, He intends for His people to be led by Him through the vehicle of PRAYER. As we trust and obey Him, we begin to understand HOW, WHEN, WHAT, and WHERE the Lord WORKS in relation to PRAYER. Doesn't that make you want to PRAY more? Why? Because remember...

"PRAYER WORKS if you WORK it"!

THE KIND OF PRAYER THAT MOVES THE HAND OF GOD

Introduction: Not every prayer, "Moves the Hand of God." For example, the following do not:

Praying with impure motives:

> *Ye lust, and have not: ye kill, and desire to have, and cannot obtain: ye fight and war, yet ye have not, because ye ask not* (Jas. 4:2).

Praying with unconfessed sin:

> *If I regard iniquity in my heart, the Lord will not hear me* (Psa. 66:18).

But when the right conditions are met—confessing sin and praying with pure motives—answers come raining down from heaven. By the way, prayer originates in heaven according to the will of God the Father. Meanwhile, God the Son—at His right hand, intercedes for every believer (Rom. 8:34). And finally, the third person of the trinity—God the Holy Spirit, helps our infirmities with groanings, which cannot be uttered because He makes intercession for the saints, according to the will of God (Rom. 8:26-27).

In the passage selected for today's devotion, there is a "Dark Side," and a "Bright Side." After being delivered from slavery in EGYPT, the Israelites are on their way to the promised land—which God gave Abraham, Isaac, Jacob and their descendants. Moses climbs up Mt. Sinai to meet with God and to receive the Ten Commandments. However, down below, the Israelites have a case of spiritual amnesia. They forget to trust in Jehovah God, and make a golden calf. This was

NOT GOOD! And of all people, Aaron helps facilitate this lascivious event.

Have you had trouble trusting in God lately? Is He not answering quick enough for you? Are you trying to get a word to calm your nerves from any source?

1. The DARK SIDE!

> *And when the people saw that Moses delayed to come down out of the mount, the people gathered themselves together unto Aaron, and said unto him, Up, make us gods, which shall go before us; for as for this Moses, the man that brought us up out of the land of Egypt, we wot not what is become of him. And Aaron said unto them, Break off the golden earrings, which are in the ears of your wives, of your sons, and of your daughters, and bring them unto me. And all the people brake off the golden earrings which were in their ears, and brought them unto Aaron. And he received them at their hand, and fashioned it with a graving tool, after he had made it a molten calf: and they said, These be thy gods, O Israel, which brought thee up out of the land of Egypt. And when Aaron saw it, he built an altar before it; and Aaron made proclamation, and said, To morrow is a feast to the LORD. And they rose up early on the morrow, and offered burnt offerings, and brought peace offerings; and the people sat down to eat and to drink, and rose up to play* (Exo. 32:1-6).

Learning Lessons:

- When you are TEMPTED to be IMPATIENT, WATCH OUT for falling into IDOLATRY (v. 1, 2-4).
- When you are TEMPTED to "do something," don't listen to the crowd... because they will lead you into APOSTASY (v. 5-6).

2. The BRIGHT SIDE!

> *And the LORD said unto Moses, Go, get thee down; for thy people, which thou broughtest out of the land of Egypt, have corrupted themselves: They have turned aside quickly out of the way which I commanded them: they have made them a molten calf, and have worshipped it, and have sacrificed thereunto, and said, These be thy gods, O Israel, which have brought thee up out of the land of Egypt. And the LORD said unto Moses, I have seen this people, and, behold, it is a stiffnecked people: Now therefore let me alone, that my wrath may wax hot against them, and that I may consume them: and I will make of thee a great nation. And Moses besought the LORD his God, and said, LORD, why doth thy wrath wax hot against thy people, which thou hast brought forth out of the land of Egypt with great power, and with a mighty hand? Wherefore should the Egyptians speak, and say, For mischief did he bring them out, to slay them in the mountains, and to consume them from the face of the earth? Turn from thy fierce wrath, and repent of this evil against thy people. Remember Abraham, Isaac, and Israel, thy servants, to whom thou swarest by thine own self, and saidst unto them, I will multiply your seed as the stars of heaven, and all this land that I have spoken of will I give unto your seed, and they shall inherit it for ever. And the LORD repented of the evil which he thought to do unto his people* (Exo. 32:7-14).

Learning Lesson:

- God is just. He must deal with sin (v. 7-10). Watch out! Get back!!

    ...Now therefore let me alone, that my wrath may wax hot against them, and that I may consume them: and I will make of

thee a great nation (v. 10).

Intercessory prayer can be POWERFUL! With the right motives, it can, "MOVE the HAND of GOD"!

So Moses interceded for the people with PREVAILING PRAYER!

> *...And Moses besought the LORD his God, and said, LORD, why doth thy wrath wax hot against thy people, which thou hast brought forth out of the land of Egypt with great power, and with a mighty hand? Wherefore should the Egyptians speak, and say, For mischief did he bring them out, to slay them in the mountains, and to consume them from the face of the earth? Turn from thy fierce wrath, and repent of this evil against thy people. Remember Abraham, Isaac, and Israel, thy servants, to whom thou swarest by thine own self, and saidst unto them, I will multiply your seed as the stars of heaven, and all this land that I have spoken of will I give unto your seed, and they shall inherit it for ever* (v. 11-13).

Will you intercede for someone who is not a Christian, someone who is backslidden, or just a brother or sister in need today?

Conclusion: Because of Moses' prevailing prayer, which "MOVED the PROVIDENTIAL HAND" of the Lord—God's fierce judgement was restrained. *"And the LORD repented of the evil which he thought to do unto his people"* (Exo. 32:14). The word "repent" is nacham (naw-kham'), which means to be sorry, to console oneself. Browns Commentary defines the word in this way: be sorry, rue, suffer grief, repent, of one's own doings. It is difficult to fully understand that God would change His mind. In this Pastor's opinion, it appears that God's perfect will was to bring His people into Canaan land; however, due to their disobedience, the wrath of God was stirred. Finding a man after His own heart—Moses, who was willing to PRAY and STAND in the GAP (Ezek. 22:30), was the key to the heart of God. Consequently, the Lord spared some of the people even though many of them were destroyed. What a powerful example of how PRAYER CHANGES THINGS! Oh yeah... PRAYER changes me and you!! Let's PRAY!

PERSEVERANCE IN PRAYER

Introduction: Does Jesus honor "Persevering Prayer"? You tell me! Throughout His earthly life, Jesus seemed to emphasize to His followers to be persistent in prayer. In fact, not only did He illustrate this truth in the Garden of Gethsemane, but He also demonstrated this principle in that "Golden Prayer" recorded in the seventeenth chapter of the gospel of John. In this passage of Scripture, Luke records the words of Jesus.

And he spake a parable unto them to this end, that men ought always to pray, and not to faint (Luke 18:1).

1. When the answer does not come immediately, do not GIVE UP, keep praying!

Saying, There was in a city a judge, which feared not God, neither regarded man: And there was a widow in that city; and she came unto him, saying, Avenge me of mine adversary. And he would not for a while (Luke 18:2-3).

Teaching on prayer in the sermon on the mount, Jesus urged His disciples to be consistent in prayer.

Ask, and it shall be given you; seek, and ye shall find; knock, and it shall be opened unto you: For every one that asketh receiveth; and he that seeketh findeth; and to him that knocketh it shall be opened. Or what man is there of you, whom if his son ask bread, will he give him a stone? Or if he ask a fish, will he give him a serpent? If ye then, being evil, know how to give good gifts unto your children, how much more shall your Father which is in heaven give good things to them that ask him? (Matt. 7:7-8).

Interesting to note, the verbs "ask, seek, and knock" are all in the present tense... meaning ask and keep on asking, etc. While it is true, our Father knows our need before we ask, yet He desires for His children to come to Him and depend on Him.

Have you "GIVEN UP" on prayer? Feel like quitting? Unanswered? Gotten discouraged? Confused? Have you resolved in your heart our Heavenly Father knows best?

2. When the devil and others who oppose you want you to GIVE IN, keep praying!

> *But afterward he said within himself, Though I fear not God, nor regard man; Yet because this widow troubleth me, I will avenge her, lest by her continual coming she weary me* (Luke 18:4-5).

The enemy lies! After twenty-one days, Daniel was told by God, that He heard his prayer from day one.

3. When your FAITH in answered PRAYER feels like GIVING OUT, keep praying!

> *And the Lord said, Hear what the unjust judge saith. And shall not God avenge his own elect, which cry day and night unto him, though he bear long with them? I tell you that he will avenge them speedily. Nevertheless when the Son of man cometh, shall he find faith on the earth?* (Luke 18:6-8).

Paul prayed for the removal of the *"thorn in his flesh"*...not once, not twice, but three times. And yet, the Lord's answer came back… *"My grace is sufficient"* (2 Cor. 12:9-12).

Conclusion: God answers prayer according to His will, and for His glory. These words should encourage every CHRISTian. Jesus is teaching His disciples, and us, to not GIVE UP PRAYING! But to keep GIVING OUT!

WRONG THINKING = WRONG PRAYING

Introduction: What are you thinking? Is your thinking affecting your praying? How are you thinking? Why are you thinking that way? Do you need to change your thinking? But how? This devotion will share biblical insights on how the Holy Spirit changes our thinking.

1. Jesus starts with the HEART!

   Do not ye yet understand, that whatsoever entereth in at the mouth goeth into the belly, and is cast out into the draught? But those things which proceed out of the mouth come forth from the heart; and they defile the man. For out of the heart proceed evil thoughts, murders, adulteries, fornications, thefts, false witness, blasphemies: These are the things which defile a man: but to eat with unwashen hands defileth not a man (Matt 15:17-20).

   And he said, That which cometh out of the man, that defileth the man. For from within, out of the heart of men, proceed evil thoughts, adulteries, fornications, murders, thefts, covetousness, wickedness, deceit, lasciviousness, an evil eye, blasphemy, pride, foolishness: All these evil things come from within, and defile the man (Mark 7:20-23).

Do you need a "change of heart"?

To attempt to change our thinking and praying without allowing Jesus Christ to change our heart will cause us to have a double mind. Why not ask Jesus right now for a change of heart by His Holy Spirit?

Jesus... change my heart... from ingratitude to gratefulness... from lustful thoughts to biblical truth... from anger and bitterness to love and forgiveness.

2. Jesus starts with the HEART then goes to the HEAD!

Paul, while in prison, writes the following:

> *Finally, brethren, whatsoever things are true, whatsoever things are honest, whatsoever things are just, whatsoever things are pure, whatsoever things are lovely, whatsoever things are of good report; if there be any virtue, and if there be any praise, think on these things. Those things, which ye have both learned, and received, and heard, and seen in me, do: and the God of peace shall be with you* (Phil. 4:8-9).

Solomon, the man who asked for wisdom from God writes,

> *For as he thinketh in his heart, so is he: Eat and drink, saith he to thee; but his heart is not with thee* (Prov 23:7).

The best way to change our "STINKING THINKING" into JOYFUL LIVING is through the power of the resurrection of Jesus Christ!

Conclusion: A change of heart is first. Digesting TRUTH that TRANSFORMS is next. Righteous thinking produces Spirit-filled praying.

PASS THE PRAYERS PLEASE

Introduction: Anybody need prayer? We all do. Are you praying for someone today? Who? Who do you need to add to your prayer list? How many people are lifting you up? Is intercessory prayer mentioned in the Bible? Where?

1. Did you know James writes in his epistle about praying for others?

   Confess your faults one to another, and pray one for another, that ye may be healed. The effectual fervent prayer of a righteous man availeth much (Jas. 5:16).

The word "healed" is iaomai (ee-ah'-om-ahee), which means I heal, generally of the physical, sometimes of spiritual, disease.

Let's consider what this does not mean. This does not mean we need a priest, a pope or a preacher to get to God. Rather we can pray and confess our sins directly to our Lord; however, this does mean that as the Holy Spirit leads we can confide in a brother or sister, more specifically one that we have offended. And especially we can pray for each other!

2. Did you know Paul writes in his epistle about praying for others?

   Pray without ceasing (1 Thess. 5:17).

   I exhort therefore, that, first of all, supplications, prayers, intercessions, and giving of thanks, be made for all men (1 Tim. 2:1).

Then he lists who we should pray for.

   For kings, and for all that are in authority; that we may lead

> *a quiet and peaceable life in all godliness and honesty. For this is good and acceptable in the sight of God our Saviour* (1 Tim. 2:2-3).

Are you praying for our President? It is ok to disagree with his policies, but biblically speaking we should pray for him.

3. Did you know our Lord Jesus writes about praying for others?

> *And I say unto you, Ask, and it shall be given you; seek, and ye shall find; knock, and it shall be opened unto you. For every one that asketh receiveth; and he that seeketh findeth; and to him that knocketh it shall be opened. If a son shall ask bread of any of you that is a father, will he give him a stone? or if he ask a fish, will he for a fish give him a serpent? Or if he shall ask an egg, will he offer him a scorpion? If ye then, being evil, know how to give good gifts unto your children: how much more shall your heavenly Father give the Holy Spirit to them that ask him?* (Luke 11:9-13).

Jesus articulates the earthly example of a father and a son in comparison to our Heavenly Father and His children. Even though this is not directly related to intercession, it is in the context of prayer.

4. Did you know John writes in his epistle about prayer?

> *And this is the confidence that we have in him, that, if we ask any thing according to his will, he heareth us: And if we know that he hear us, whatsoever we ask, we know that we have the petitions that we desired of him* (1 John 5:14-15).

Obviously, there are conditions for answered prayer. For instance, There is God's will. As we intercede it is extremely important that we pray according to the will of our heavenly Father.

5. How about Abraham's willingness to intercede for Sodom and Gomorrah?

First, notice our Lord's CONDEMNATION on Sodom!

And the LORD said, Because the cry of Sodom and Gomorrah is great, and because their sin is very grievous; I will go down now, and see whether they have done altogether according to the cry of it, which is come unto me; and if not, I will know (Gen. 18:20-21).

Secondly, look at Abraham's INTERCESSION for Sodom!

And the men turned their faces from thence, and went toward Sodom: but Abraham stood yet before the LORD. And Abraham drew near, and said, Wilt thou also destroy the righteous with the wicked? Peradventure there be fifty righteous within the city: wilt thou also destroy and not spare the place for the fifty righteous that are therein? That be far from thee to do after this manner, to slay the righteous with the wicked: and that the righteous should be as the wicked, that be far from thee: Shall not the Judge of all the earth do right? And the LORD said, If I find in Sodom fifty righteous within the city, then I will spare all the place for their sakes. And Abraham answered and said, Behold now, I have taken upon me to speak unto the Lord, which am but dust and ashes: Peradventure there shall lack five of the fifty righteous: wilt thou destroy all the city for lack of five? And he said, If I find there forty and five, I will not destroy it. And he spake unto him yet again, and said, Peradventure there shall be forty found there. And he said, I will not do it for forty's sake. And he said unto him, Oh let not the Lord be angry, and I will speak: Peradventure there shall thirty be found there. And he said, I will not do it, if I find thirty there. And he said, Behold now, I have taken upon me to speak unto the Lord: Peradventure there shall be twenty found there. And he said, I will not destroy it for twenty's sake. And he said, Oh let not the Lord be angry, and I will speak yet but this once: (Gen. 18:22-32).

Lastly, check out God's RESOLUTION!

Peradventure ten shall be found there. And he said, I will not destroy it for ten's sake. And the LORD went his way, as soon as he had left communing with Abraham: and Abraham returned unto his place (Gen. 18:31-33).

Here is a great example of the power of intercession. Because of Abraham's willingness to pray on behalf of this city, our Lord was ready to spare them if there were enough righteous (light in the place).

Conclusion: I need others to pray for me. You need others to pray for you. We all need to pray for each other. So let's pray!

FIVE NON-NEGOTIABLES OF PRAYER

Introduction: Without daily output of prayer, a CHRISTian will remain an infant... or carnal.

1. Daily PRAYER!

Continue in prayer (Col 4:2).

Daily devotional prayer should include:

- Confession
- Thanksgiving
- Supplication
- Worship

How is your prayer life? Do you make a special time to talk to our Lord every day? This Pastor finds it very helpful to start off the day with our Lord in prayer. Then throughout the day and night, we can lift up our hearts and words to our trustworthy Lord and Savior Jesus Christ. He knows our needs anyway. But His desire is to have a relationship with us. How is your relationship with Jesus today?

2. Special PRAYER for others!

Praying always with all prayer and supplication in the Spirit, and watching thereunto with all perseverance and supplication for all saints (Eph. 6:18).

Being in a right relationship with Jesus or staying connected, allows believers to intercede for others... this includes:

- Marriages
- Families
- Those who are not CHRISTians
- Our nation
- Churches, pastors, ministry
- Health needs, etc...

Do you pray regularly for the needs listed above? Why not start? Why not get you a prayer book and start recording answered prayers. It will encourage you, as well as build your faith in a FAITHFUL God!

    Conclusion: Is prayer a priority to you? Or has it become a spare tire, just when you need it. Do not forget, the purpose of prayer is not just getting from our God what we want, but rather it is establishing a relationship that will last throughout eternity!

SPIRITUAL LESSONS WITH PRAYER PARTNERS

Introduction: Do you have a prayer partner? How important is it for two or more to intercede together? With two or more fighting the spiritual battle, victory can be obtained. In this devotion, the significance of having more than one on your team is seen; and furthermore, the VICTORY is accomplished.

1. Look who is Jonathan's prayer partner—armor bearer!

> *Now it came to pass upon a day, that Jonathan the son of Saul said unto the young man that bare his armour, Come, and let us go over to the Philistines' garrison, that is on the other side. But he told not his father* (1 Sam. 14:1).

Notice how they agreed together. There must be UNITY before there is VICTORY!

2. Look why Jonathan needs a prayer partner—armor bearer!

> *And between the passages, by which Jonathan sought to go over unto the Philistines' garrison, there was a sharp rock on the one side, and a sharp rock on the other side: and the name of the one was Bozez, and the name of the other Seneh. The forefront of the one was situate northward over against Michmash, and the other southward over against Gibeah. And Jonathan said to the young man that bare his armour, Come, and let us go over unto the garrison of these uncircumcised: it may be that the LORD will work for us: for there is no restraint to the LORD to save by many or by few* (1 Sam. 14:4-6).

Did you see the FAITH demonstrated by Jonathan? Without some

MATURITY of FAITH and TRUST, there can be no VICTORY!

3. Look how God gave Jonathan and his prayer partner—armor bearer—the victory!

> *And his armourbearer said unto him, Do all that is in thine heart: turn thee; behold, I am with thee according to thy heart. Then said Jonathan, Behold, we will pass over unto these men, and we will discover ourselves unto them. If they say thus unto us, Tarry until we come to you; then we will stand still in our place, and will not go up unto them. But if they say thus, Come up unto us; then we will go up: for the LORD hath delivered them into our hand: and this shall be a sign unto us. And both of them discovered themselves unto the garrison of the Philistines: and the Philistines said, Behold, the Hebrews come forth out of the holes where they had hid themselves. And the men of the garrison answered Jonathan and his armourbearer, and said, Come up to us, and we will shew you a thing. And Jonathan said unto his armourbearer, Come up after me: for the LORD hath delivered them into the hand of Israel. And Jonathan climbed up upon his hands and upon his feet, and his armourbearer after him: and they fell before Jonathan; and his armourbearer slew after him. And that first slaughter, which Jonathan and his armourbearer made, was about twenty men, within as it were an half acre of land, which a yoke of oxen might plow* (1 Sam 14:7-14).

What did you think about their plan of DIVERSITY?

Conclusion: Without UNITY, MATURITY, and DIVERSITY in our prayers, we can see there will be NO VICTORY! But once we get on the same page and exercise reliance upon the Lord as He guides, acknowledging that He may change our strategy, then along with our prayer partner—we can celebrate the VICTORY!

A GREAT PRAYER FOR YOU

Introduction: How can we pray for others, each other? Many claim to be praying. But in what ways? First, don't forget confession. Then do a thorough job of cleansing. Next, get ready for the calling. Will you make this a prayer for someone today? Technically speaking, Paul prayed the following prayer for the believers in Ephesus. Just as they needed it—due to the temple of Dianna, we need it because of the idolatry and immorality in our world.

Make the following a prayer for someone "special":

1. "Lord" may they experience the "Riches of Your GLORY"!

   That he would grant you, according to the riches of his glory... (Eph. 3:16).

The glory of God is the ultimate objective.

2. "Lord" may they experience the "Riches of Your GLORY" and be "Strengthened by Your might in their inner being"!

   That he would grant you, according to the riches of his glory, to be strengthened with might by his Spirit in the inner man (Eph. 3:16).

Give them "Strength" for the journey.

3. "Lord" may they experience the "Riches of Your GRACE" & be "Strengthened by Your might in their inner being"...and then Lord may they be "Rooted and grounded in Your LOVE"!

   That Christ may dwell in your hearts by faith; that ye, being rooted and grounded in love (Eph. 3:17).

The Love of Christ motivates us!

4. "Lord" may they experience the "Riches of Your GRACE" & be "Strengthened by Your might in their inner being"...and then Lord may they be "Rooted and grounded in Your LOVE....and then finally may they be "FILLED with all of Your FULLNESS"!

And to know the love of Christ, which passeth knowledge, that ye might be filled with all the fulness of God (Eph. 3:19).

To be "filled with the fullness of God" means to be under His control.

Conclusion: Will you pray this for me? And I will pray this for you!

PRAYING IN FAITH

Introduction: Are you praying in FAITH? Some pray in FEAR! What does it mean to pray in FAITH? Consider the following:

1. Jesus taught it!

> *And Jesus answering saith unto them, Have faith in God. For verily I say unto you, That whosoever shall say unto this mountain, Be thou removed, and be thou cast into the sea; and shall not doubt in his heart, but shall believe that those things which he saith shall come to pass; he shall have whatsoever he saith. Therefore I say unto you, What things soever ye desire, when ye pray, believe that ye receive them, and ye shall have them* (Mark 11:22-24).

In other words, if we are not praying in faith, we cannot please our Lord (Heb. 11:6).

2. James bought it!

> *Is any among you afflicted? let him pray. Is any merry? let him sing psalms. Is any sick among you? let him call for the elders of the church; and let them pray over him, anointing him with oil in the name of the Lord: And the prayer of faith shall save the sick, and the Lord shall raise him up; and if he have committed sins, they shall be forgiven him. Confess your faults one to another, and pray one for another, that ye may be healed. The effectual fervent prayer of a righteous man availeth much* (Jas. 5:13-16).

This means praying in the will of God.

3. The devil fought it!

> *And the Lord said, Simon, Simon, behold, Satan hath desired to have you, that he may sift you as wheat: But I have prayed for thee, that thy faith fail not: and when thou art converted, strengthen thy brethren* (Luke 22:30-31).

If the devil can block our prayers he will! Is the devil working in you? Jesus overcame him. We can too—through Jesus!

Conclusion: Now that we've demonstrated that "Praying in FAITH" is TAUGHT by Jesus, BOUGHT by James, and finally, FOUGHT by the devil—the question remains. Are we praying in FAITH? According to the will of God and the Word of God? All for the Glory of God?!

PRAYER ARSENAL AGAINST THE ENEMY

Introduction: Prayer is the catalyst that *"initiates and activates"* the POWER of our Mighty God—Jesus Christ! King Jehoshaphat witnessed firsthand this principle. There are great "Lessons to Learn" from our Scripture today.

1. When stricken with FEAR, we can TURN to our Lord!

> *It came to pass after this also, that the children of Moab, and the children of Ammon, and with them other beside the Ammonites, came against Jehoshaphat to battle. Then there came some that told Jehoshaphat, saying, There cometh a great multitude against thee from beyond the sea on this side Syria; and, behold, they be in Hazazontamar, which is Engedi. And Jehoshaphat feared, and set himself to seek the LORD, and proclaimed a fast throughout all Judah* (2 Chron. 20:1-3).

Are you living in FEAR? FEAR for the FUTURE? FEAR for your FAMILY? FEAR over your FINANCES? Jesus reminds us not to fear... not to be afraid. Attacks from the enemy will come. BE AWARE. BE READY.

2. When we are AFRAID, we can TURN to JESUS and TALK to JESUS!

> *And Judah gathered themselves together, to ask help of the LORD: even out of all the cities of Judah they came to seek the LORD. And Jehoshaphat stood in the congregation of Judah and Jerusalem, in the house of the LORD, before the new court, And said, O LORD God of our fathers, art not thou God in heaven? and rulest not thou over all the kingdoms of the heathen? and in thine hand is there not power and might, so that none is able to*

withstand thee? Art not thou our God, who didst drive out the inhabitants of this land before thy people Israel, and gavest it to the seed of Abraham thy friend for ever? And they dwelt therein, and have built thee a sanctuary therein for thy name, saying, If, when evil cometh upon us, as the sword, judgment, or pestilence, or famine, we stand before this house, and in thy presence, (for thy name is in this house,) and cry unto thee in our affliction, then thou wilt hear and help. And now, behold, the children of Ammon and Moab and mount Seir, whom thou wouldest not let Israel invade, when they came out of the land of Egypt, but they turned from them, and destroyed them not; Behold, I say, how they reward us, to come to cast us out of thy possession, which thou hast given us to inherit. O our God, wilt thou not judge them? for we have no might against this great company that cometh against us; neither know we what to do: but our eyes are upon thee. And all Judah stood before the LORD, with their little ones, their wives, and their children (2 Chron. 20:4-13).

BE ARMED with prayer. TURNING and TALKING to JESUS levels the playing field!

3. When we are AFRAID, we can TURN to JESUS, TALK to JESUS, and TRUST in JESUS!

Then upon Jahaziel the son of Zechariah, the son of Benaiah, the son of Jeiel, the son of Mattaniah, a Levite of the sons of Asaph, came the Spirit of the LORD in the midst of the congregation; And he said, Hearken ye, all Judah, and ye inhabitants of Jerusalem, and thou king Jehoshaphat, Thus saith the LORD unto you, Be not afraid nor dismayed by reason of this great multitude; for the battle is not yours, but God's. To morrow go ye down against them: behold, they come up by the cliff of Ziz; and ye shall find them at the end of the brook, before the wilderness of Jeruel. Ye

> *shall not need to fight in this battle: set yourselves, stand ye still, and see the salvation of the LORD with you, O Judah and Jerusalem: fear not, nor be dismayed; to morrow go out against them: for the LORD will be with you* (2 Chron. 20:14-17).

Realizing our dependency upon our Creator is the first step. Then co-operating with Him RELEASES His power.

4. When we are AFRAID, we can TURN to JESUS , TALK to JESUS, TRUST in JESUS, and TRIUMPH in JESUS!

> *Then they returned, every man of Judah and Jerusalem, and Jehoshaphat in the forefront of them, to go again to Jerusalem with joy; for the LORD had made them to rejoice over their enemies. And they came to Jerusalem with psalteries and harps and trumpets unto the house of the LORD. And the fear of God was on all the kingdoms of those countries, when they had heard that the LORD fought against the enemies of Israel* (2 Chron. 20:27-28).

5. JESUS always WINS! He is LORD!!

Conclusion: When we are FEARFUL and AFRAID because of the attacks of the enemy—we can TURN, TALK, TRUST, and TRIUMPH in JESUS!

Will you do that now?

ENGAGING THE ENEMY THRU PRAYER

Introduction: Can you tell that Satan has people held in captivity today? Sadly, they do not realize it. While bound down in chains of sin and rebellion, he manipulates their mind, will, and emotions. Yet, there is power in PRAYER over the enemy. But ONLY because Jesus Christ has defeated Satan. And ultimately, Satan will be thrown in the lake of fire. That is why he knows his time is short. Meanwhile, how can we help people get FREE from the control of the enemy?

Here are a few biblical insights:

1. Breaking FREE from the devil calls for INTERCESSORY PRAYER!

> *Praying always with all prayer and supplication in the Spirit, and watching thereunto with all perseverance and supplication for all saints* (Eph. 6:17-18).

JESUS PRAYS for His followers.

> *And the Lord said, Simon, Simon, behold, Satan hath desired to have you, that he may sift you as wheat: But I have prayed for thee, that thy faith fail not: and when thou art converted, strengthen thy brethren* (Luke 22:30-31).

Praise the Lord! Not only is Jesus interceding, but we also are instructed to PRAY against the enemy. Are you? Check out the next demonically-driven case of a MAD-MAN that was turned into a GLAD-MAN.

2. Breaking FREE from MENTAL and PHYSICAL torment by the devil calls for INTERCESSORY POWER!

And when he was come out of the ship, immediately there met him out of the tombs a man with an unclean spirit, Who had his dwelling among the tombs; and no man could bind him, no, not with chains: Because that he had been often bound with fetters and chains, and the chains had been plucked asunder by him, and the fetters broken in pieces: neither could any man tame him. And always, night and day, he was in the mountains, and in the tombs, crying, and cutting himself with stones. But when he saw Jesus afar off, he ran and worshipped him, And cried with a loud voice, and said, What have I to do with thee, Jesus, thou Son of the most high God? I adjure thee by God, that thou torment me not. For he said unto him, Come out of the man, thou unclean spirit. And he asked him, What is thy name? And he answered, saying, My name is Legion: for we are many. And he besought him much that he would not send them away out of the country. Now there was there nigh unto the mountains a great herd of swine feeding. And all the devils besought him, saying, Send us into the swine, that we may enter into them. And forthwith Jesus gave them leave. And the unclean spirits went out, and entered into the swine: and the herd ran violently down a steep place into the sea, (they were about two thousand;) and were choked in the sea (Mark 5:1-13).

This man was possessed with many demons. Only Jesus could help him. By the way, our task does not rely upon our own strength. Instead, our POWER to stand and pray comes from JESUS CHRIST. Please, do not ever try to engage the enemy without the POWER of Jesus Christ!

3. Breaking FREE from MENTAL, PHYSICAL, and SPIRITUAL torment by the devil calls for INTERCESSION, which leads to TRANSFORMATION!

And they come to Jesus, and see him that was possessed with the devil, and had the legion, sitting, and clothed, and in his right mind: and they were afraid. And they that saw it told them how it befell to him that was possessed with the devil, and also concerning the swine. And they began to pray him to depart out of their coasts. And when he was come into the ship, he that had been possessed with the devil prayed him that he might be with him. Howbeit Jesus suffered him not, but saith unto him, Go home to thy friends, and tell them how great things the Lord hath done for thee, and hath had compassion on thee. And he departed, and began to publish in Decapolis how great things Jesus had done for him: and all men did marvel (Mark 5:15-20).

Did you notice the instantaneous CHANGE? That is the POWER of God!

Conclusion: I wonder who was praying for this man. Perhaps, at least his family. Maybe more. Either way, JESUS set him FREE! Remember, Jesus is praying for us and instructs us to pray for others. Especially those that are bound down by Satan. We need not be afraid—but neither ignorant of Satan's devices. Why? Because Jesus is LORD!

STRIVING IN PRAYER

Introduction: Is PRAYER WORK? Does PRAYER WORK? It works, if you work it! How does it work? Paul encourages other believers to join him in prayer. Check it out:

1. The Power of Prayer!

> *Now I beseech you, brethren, for the Lord Jesus Christ's sake, and for the love of the Spirit, that ye strive together with me in your prayers to God for me* (Rom. 15:30).

The word "strive" is sunagonizomai (soon-ag-o-nid'-zom-ahee), which means I struggle in company with, aid. When we get under the burden to pray for others, it can be taxing, but rewarding!

2. The Purpose of Prayer!

> *That I may be delivered from them that do not believe in Judaea; and that my service which I have for Jerusalem may be accepted of the saints* (Rom. 15:31).

There is a goal in Paul's prayer. It is for God's glory, but for the Church's good.

3. The Peace in Prayer!

> *That I may come unto you with joy by the will of God, and may with you be refreshed. Now the God of peace be with you all. Amen* (Rom. 15:32-33).

Everyone needs refreshing! All of us need the peace of God.

Conclusion: This passage of Scripture reveals the multipurpose for prayer. It's powerful! It brings peace! It brings provision!

PRAYER LIKE INCENSE

Introduction: Are you praying in FAITH? Either we can WORRY or PRAY! Prayer is the cure for CARE! But how does God view prayer? Simply put. It is all about a RELATIONSHIP. Without communication, there would not be much of a relationship. So pray. Pray when you feel like it; pray when you don't feel like it; and pray UNTIL you feel like it!

I love the picture of how God views prayer in Revelation Chapter Eight. Even though technically speaking—this is during the tribulation when the judgments of God (the seven trumpets) are being released on the earth, practically—prayers are being offered to the throne of grace (Heb. 4:14-16).

Check it out.

1. Saints are praying!

> *And another angel came and stood at the altar, having a golden censer; and there was given unto him much incense, that he should offer it with the prayers of all saints upon the golden altar which was before the throne* (Rev. 8:3).

Not only are we supposed to offer petitions to our heavenly Father, but we are also to confess our sins. This opens up the door to the throne.

2. Prayers are ascending!

> *And the smoke of the incense, which came with the prayers of the saints, ascended up before God out of the angel's hand* (Rev. 8:4).

After the door of the throne is opened, then we approach the mercy seat as it were thru the blood of the everlasting covenant. Jesus Christ made a way!

3. Prayers are answered!

> *And the angel took the censer, and filled it with fire of the altar, and cast it into the earth: and there were voices, and thunderings, and lightnings, and an earthquake* (Rev. 8:5).

When prayer is brought to the throne in faith—answers come in God's timing. Be patient.

Conclusion: Remember—the purpose of PRAYER is to develop a RELATIONSHIP with JESUS. Because of His sacrifice, we are able to approach His throne.

> *Having therefore, brethren, boldness to enter into the holiest by the blood of Jesus, By a new and living way, which he hath consecrated for us, through the veil, that is to say, his flesh; And having an high priest over the house of God; Let us draw near with a true heart in full assurance of faith, having our hearts sprinkled from an evil conscience, and our bodies washed with pure water. Let us hold fast the profession of our faith without wavering; (for he is faithful that promised* (Heb. 10:19-23).

Go ahead. Pray.

TEACH US TO PRAY

Introduction: How is your prayer life? Occasionally, it does me good to take inventory on my prayer life? Do you need to? Let's face it, the purpose of prayer is to have a relationship with the God of the Bible... by talking and listening to Him. This starts as we turn from our sin, trust in Jesus' precious cleansing blood, and receive Him as our Lord and Savior. Remember the "SWEET HOUR of PRAYER." Our culture has changed it to "SWEET MINUTE of PRAYER" (guess that's better than nothing). Is that the way to really build a meaningful LOVE RELATIONSHIP? So why and how should we pray?

1. Why should we PRAY? *"Lord, teach us to pray..."*

   - Why? Because we have not because we ask not.

     Ye lust, and have not: ye kill, and desire to have, and cannot obtain: ye fight and war, yet ye have not, because ye ask not (Jas. 4:2).

   - Why? To keep us from falling into temptation.

     Watch and pray, that ye enter not into temptation: the spirit indeed is willing but the flesh is weak (Matt. 26:41).

   - Why? Because we have an enemy.

     Deliver us from evil... (Matt 6:13).

2. How should we PRAY? *"Lord, teach us to pray..."*

   - Pray in Jesus' name.

     And whatsoever ye shall ask in my name, that will I do, that the Father may be glorified in the Son. If ye shall ask any thing in my name, I will do it (John 14:13-14).

- Pray according to the will of God.

  And this is the confidence that we have in him, that, if we ask any thing according to his will, he heareth us. And if we know that he hear us, whatsoever we ask, we know that we have the petitions that we desired of him (1 John 5:14-15).

- Pray in faith.

  But I say unto you, It shall be more tolerable for Tyre and Sidon at the day of judgment, than for you. And thou, Capernaum, which art exalted unto heaven, shalt be brought down to hell: for if the mighty works, which have been done in thee, had been done in Sodom, it would have remained until this day. But I say unto you, That it shall be more tolerable for the land of Sodom in the day of judgment, than for thee (Matt. 11:22-24).

- Pray for God's glory.

  These words spake Jesus, and lifted up his eyes to heaven, and said, Father, the hour is come; glorify thy Son, that thy Son also may glorify thee: (John 17:1).

Conclusion: Quantity and quality go hand in hand when it comes to praying. Do you want just 30 seconds a day/week with those you love? Or more like 30 minutes to an hour or more? How does our Heavenly Father feel when we just go to him when we've got a "flat tire"—or when we want Him to heal us or get us out of trouble? That's ok as long as we have a RELATIONSHIP with Him. But as a parent or a friend, we want to spend time with those we love. We've all enrolled in this SCHOOL of PRAYER... graduation is when we get to heaven!

So... *"Lord, teach us to pray."*

THE POWER OF PRAYING FOR ONE ANOTHER

Introduction: Is there really POWER in prayer? Have you prayed for anybody today? Finish this statement: When we pray for one another there is _____? James, the half-brother of Jesus, gives us (believers) three instructions for praying for each other.

1. When should we PRAY?

> *Is there any among you afflicted? Let him pray. Is any merry? Let him sing psalms. Is any sick among you: let him call for the elders of the church; and let them pray over him, anointing him with oil in the name of the Lord* (Jas. 5:13-14).

- When we face adversity or are "afflicted" (kak-op-ath-eh-o), which means to suffer, endure evils (hardships, troubles).

- When we are "sick" (as-then-eh-o), which means to be weak, feeble, to be without strength.

2. How should we PRAY?

> *And the prayer of faith shall save the sick, and the Lord shall raise him up, and if he hath committed sins, they shall be forgiven him* (Jas. 5:15).

God answers the PRAYER of faith.

3. Whose PRAYERS have GREAT strength?

> *Confess your faults one to another, that ye may be healed: The effectual fervent prayer of a righteous man availeth much* (Jas. 5:16).

- "Effectual fervent" (en-erg-eh-o), which means to be operative, be at work, put forth power.
- "Availeth" (is-khoo-o), which means to be strong, to have power, strength to overcome.

Conclusion: Would you agree? The PRAYER of faith brings both mental and physical healing... according to the WORD of God and the WILL of God. Faith is cultivated by a need, planted by a promise, and harvested by the Lord of the Harvest—Jesus Christ. Do you know anybody who needs PRAYER?

PRAYER AT THE RIVER

Introduction: Have you met Lydia? This morning a friend sent me a picture of his newborn granddaughter. Guess what his son and his wife named her? Lydia. Wouldn't you like to meet the Lydia of the Bible? She was both a wealthy woman and a wise woman. Check out how our Lord Jesus orchestrated His will in this unique situation.

The following questions tell the story:

1. Where?

> *And on the sabbath we went out of the city by a river side, where prayer was wont to be made; and we sat down, and spake unto the women which resorted thither* (Acts 16:13).

Imagine the scene... praying by a river. There is just something "PEACEFUL" about a river. Prayer can be offered ANYWHERE, because our God is EVERYWHERE!

2. Who?

> *And a certain woman named Lydia, a seller of purple, of the city of Thyatira, which worshipped God, heard us* (Acts 16:14).

Prayer unites believers.

Interestingly to note, Lydia heard Paul praying. You never know who may be listening. Evidently, Lydia was a businesswoman, a seller of purple—an expensive dye. She seemed to be somewhat religious. Or at least she was seeking the Lord.

3. What?

> ...whose heart the Lord opened, that she attended unto the things which were spoken of Paul. And when she was baptized, and her household (Acts 16:14-15).

Praise God! Jesus opened her heart through the vehicle of prayer and by His Spirit. Her whole house was saved!! And to demonstrate their obedience—they were baptized.

4. How?

> And when she was baptized, and her household, she besought us, saying, If ye have judged me to be faithful to the Lord, come into my house, and abide there. And she constrained us (Acts 16:15).

The proof of her conversion to Jesus Christ was quickly acknowledged by all in her willingness to extend hospitality to Paul and Silas. We are not saved by WORKS, but if we are saved—there will be some WORKS!

Conclusion: What a beautiful picture of the power of prayer and the quickening of the Holy Spirit in a religious lady who needed a relationship with Jesus. Doesn't this motivate you to want to pray and obey more?

DO YOU PRAY SELF-RIGHTEOUSLY OR CHRIST-RIGHTEOUSLY?

Introduction: How do you pray? Jesus is listening. Do you realize that some people go down as being justified when they pray, according to our Lord, whereas others when they pray are proud and therefore unheard. How do we know that? Jesus gives us this analogy of two men who went to the temple to pray. Here is what He said:

And he spake this parable unto certain which trusted in themselves that they were righteous, and despised others... Two men went up into the temple to pray; the one a Pharisee and the other a publican (Luke 18:9-10).

1. A GOOD man needed to lose his GOODNESS in order to be clothed in Jesus' RIGHTEOUSNESS!

The Pharisee stood and prayed thus with himself, God, I thank thee, that I am not as other men are, extortioners, unjust, adulterers, or even as this publican. I fast twice in the week, I give tithes of all that I possess (Luke 18:11-12).

Did you notice his prayer consisted of telling God how "GOOD" he was compared to other people? Sometimes, unknowingly, we commit the same mistake. Deep down in our heart is PRIDE and SELF-RIGHTEOUSNESS. Secretly, we feel a little better than other people; i.e., I read my Bible, go to church, don't drink, smoke, or steal—but our Lord searches our heart. Have you been praying self-righteously lately? Time for a CHECK UP!

2. A BAD man humbled himself and was justified with Christ's RIGHTEOUSNESS!

> *And the publican, standing afar off, would not lift up so much as his eyes unto heaven, but smote upon his breast, saying, God be merciful to me a sinner* (Luke 18:13).

This man saw himself as Jesus saw him… unrighteous outside of Christ's righteousness. Yet, that made him a candidate to be clothed in Christ's righteousness. After conversion, we are made righteous in Jesus Christ. However, even the "BEST of CHRISTians" can develop a self-righteous attitude. How do you pray? What response would Jesus give toward your prayers and my prayers?

    Conclusion: Listen to Jesus Christ's evaluation of the publican—the second man who prayed.

> *I tell you, this man went down to his house justified rather than the other: for every one that exalteth himself shall be abased; and he that humbleth himself shall be exalted* (Luke 18:14).

The obvious conclusion is to CHECK UP on your prayer life. See what Jesus thinks. You can't go wrong then. If you are wrong—let the Lord make it right.

WHEN GOD SAYS NO TO OUR PRAYERS

Introduction: Do you think that every time we pray earnestly God answers with what we ask? Sadly, many CHRISTians believe that. And if the Lord does not give them what they want, they stop praying and stop trusting. However, we can deduce from this Scripture today that prayer is both a growing experience and a trusting process. Where are you at in this equation?

Paul goes from His EXALTATION—caught up to the third heaven, to his HUMILIATION and AFFLICTION—a thorn in his flesh, to his TRANSFORMATION—learning to TRUST in Jesus no matter what.

1. Paul is driven to PRAYER because of his EXALTATION!

> *...And lest I should be exalted above measure through the abundance of the revelations* (2 Cor. 12:7).

Experiencing what no mortal man had, Paul was raptured up into the third heaven. He could have shared his TESTIMONY from that point on—written best seller books, made a movie. Our Lord knows what we can handle.

3. Paul prays because he is HUMBLED through his AFFLICTION!

> *...there was given to me a thorn in the flesh, the messenger of Satan to buffet me, lest I should be exalted above measure. For this thing I besought the Lord thrice, that it might depart from me* (2 Cor. 12:7-18).

Isn't it interesting that our Lord Jesus would allow Satan to buffet Paul (to cuff, to slap with fist)? What about me and you?

3. Paul prays with strong INTERCESSION for the thorn to be removed, but his request is declined. Instead, he experiences a TRANSFORMATION because of God's GRACE!

> *For this thing I besought the Lord thrice, that it might depart from me. And he said unto me, My grace is sufficient for thee: for my strength is made perfect in weakness. Most gladly therefore will I rather glory in my infirmities, that the power of Christ may rest upon me. Therefore I take pleasure in infirmities, in reproaches, in necessities, in persecutions, in distresses for Christ's sake: for when I am weak, then am I strong* (2 Cor. 12:8-10).

Even though Paul prays (entreats/begs) earnestly for the thorn to be taken away, it doesn't happen. While refusing to remove the thorn (eye disease, malaria, etc. and a host of other speculations)—Jesus gives him His AMAZING GRACE! His GRACE is for the RACE!! It's in PLACE!!!

Conclusion: Just because we believe in the power of prayer does not mean we get everything we ask God for. In fact, we do not have the BIG PICTURE. But JESUS does! His GRACE is enough!!

CALLING DOCTOR JESUS

Introduction: Aren't you glad when you call Dr. JESUS, He doesn't tell you to press #1 to talk to Michael... or #2 to talk to Mary.

There are three reasons we ought to CALL DR. JESUS:

1. When you've got a SPIRITUAL problem, it's not a HOPELESS condition with Dr. Jesus!

And they arrived at the country of the Gadarenes, which is over against Galilee. And when he went forth to land, there met him out of the city a certain man, which had devils long time, and ware no clothes, neither abode in any house, but in the tombs. When he saw Jesus, he cried out, and fell down before him, and with a loud voice said, What have I to do with thee, Jesus, thou Son of God most high? I beseech thee, torment me not. (For he had commanded the unclean spirit to come out of the man. For oftentimes it had caught him: and he was kept bound with chains and in fetters; and he brake the bands, and was driven of the devil into the wilderness.) And Jesus asked him, saying, What is thy name? And he said, Legion: because many devils were entered into him. And they besought him that he would not command them to go out into the deep. And there was there an herd of many swine feeding on the mountain: and they besought him that he would suffer them to enter into them. And he suffered them. Then went the devils out of the man, and entered into the swine: and the herd ran violently down a steep place into the lake, and were choked. When they that fed them saw what was done, they fled, and went and told it in the city and in the country. Then they went out to see what was done; and came to Jesus, and found the man, out of whom the devils were departed, sitting at the feet of Jesus, clothed, and in his right mind: and they were afraid. They also which saw it told them by what means he that was possessed of the devils was healed. Then the whole multitude of the country of the Gadarenes round about besought him to depart from them; for they were taken with great fear: and he went up into the ship, and returned back again. Now the man out of whom the devils were departed besought him that he might be with him: but Jesus sent him away, saying, Return to thine own house, and shew how great things God hath done unto thee. And he went his way, and published throughout the whole city how great things Jesus had done unto him (Luke 8:26-39).

- Deadly demons destroy.
- Divine Deliverer delivers.
- Changes to "right mind."

2. When you've got an EMOTIONAL or PHYSICAL problem, it's not a HELPLESS case with Dr. Jesus!

And a woman having an issue of blood twelve years, which had spent all her living upon physicians, neither could be healed of any, Came behind him, and touched the border of his garment: and immediately her issue of blood stanched. And Jesus said, Who touched me? When all denied, Peter and they that were with him said, Master, the multitude throng thee and press thee, and sayest thou, Who touched me? And Jesus said, Somebody hath touched me: for I perceive that virtue is gone out of me. And when the woman saw that she was not hid, she came trembling, and falling down before him, she declared unto him before all the people for what cause she had touched him, and how she was healed immediately. And he said unto her, Daughter, be of good comfort: thy faith hath made thee whole; go in peace (Luke 8:43-48).

- A weary woman who was worn down and worried.
- She reached out and touched Jesus, and because of her "faith" she was "made whole."

3. When you've got an ETERNAL problem, it's not beyond a HEALING cure with Dr. Jesus

> *And, behold, there came a man named Jairus, and he was a ruler of the synagogue: and he fell down at Jesus' feet, and besought him that he would come into his house: For he had one only daughter, about twelve years of age, and she lay a dying. But as he went the people thronged him... While he yet spake, there cometh one from the ruler of the synagogue's house, saying to him, Thy daughter is dead; trouble not the Master. But when Jesus heard it, he answered him, saying, Fear not: believe only, and she shall be made whole. And when he came into the house, he suffered no man to go in, save Peter, and James, and John, and the father and the mother of the maiden. And all wept, and bewailed her: but he said, Weep not; she is not dead, but sleepeth. And they laughed him to scorn, knowing that she was dead. And he put them all out, and took her by the hand, and called, saying, Maid, arise. And her spirit came again, and she arose straightway: and he commanded to give her meat. And her parents were astonished: but he charged them that they should tell no man what was done* (Luke 8:41-42, 49-56).

Conclusion: With Dr. Jesus, you don't have to make an appointment days or weeks in advance. He will not send you to a specialist. Because He made us—He knows how to cure us!

LIFTING UP HOLY HANDS WITH THANKSGIVING

Introduction: C.H. Spurgeon used to say, "Prayer and Praise are cousins." Paul instructs Timothy of the importance of "Praise and Prayer." We are included. Don't forget "THANKSGIVING"! Let's see if you agree with these three challenges for all CHRISTians.

1. Will you meet me at the "Throne of God" and PRAY?

   I exhort therefore, that, first of all, supplications, prayers, intercessions, and giving of thanks, be made for all men; (1 Tim. 2:1).

   - *"Exhort"* is parakaleō, which means come alongside.
   - *"Supplication"* is deēsis, which means request, petition.
   - *"Intercession"* is enteuxis, which means falling in with, meeting with, an interview.
   - *"Thanksgiving"* is eucharistia, which means giving of thanks.

How shall we pray?

   - Supplications
   - Intercession
   - Thanksgiving

Who shall we pray for?

   - For all men, especially those in authority.

2. Will you meet me at the "Throne of God" and PRAY and then WALK like a CHRISTian?

> *For kings, and for all that are in authority; that we may lead a quiet and peaceable life in all godliness and honesty. For this is good and acceptable in the sight of God our Saviour;* (1 Tim. 2:2-3).

- The word "kings" is basileús, which means those leading other people, kings.
- The word "authority" is hyperochē, which means superiority, elevation.
- The word "quiet" is hēsýchios, which means peaceable, tranquil.
- The word "tranquil" is erēmos, which means quiet, solitary.
- The word "honesty" is semnotēs, which means seriousness, respect, gravity, holiness.

After we pray for those in authority, then we are to live peaceably and respectfully.

3. Will you meet at the "Throne of God" and PRAY, and then GO and GLOW for the GLORY of our Lord?

> *For this is good and acceptable in the sight of God our Saviour; Who will have all men to be saved, and to come unto the knowledge of the truth. For there is one God, and one mediator between God and men, the man Christ Jesus; Who gave himself a ransom for all, to be testified in due time. Whereunto I am ordained a preacher, and an apostle, (I speak the truth in Christ, and lie not;) a teacher of the Gentiles in faith and verity* (1 Tim. 2:3-7).

- Speaking of Jesus, who gave Himself a "ransom." The word "ransom" is antilytron, which means to purchase for a price.

Paul is telling Timothy and us that Jesus desires for all men to be saved because He paid for our sins.

Conclusion: In the light of what Jesus has done for us, i.e. paying for our sins, we ought to pray for all men, and especially for those in authority. Then afterwards, we are to live a peaceable life that is motivated by sharing with others how the life, death, and resurrection of Jesus Christ ought to cause us to "LIFT up HOLY HANDS with THANKSGIVING"!

I will therefore that men pray every where, lifting up holy hands, without wrath and doubting (1 Tim. 2:8).

PRAY FOR THE PEACE OF JERUSALEM

Introduction: Do you "Pray for the Peace of Jerusalem"? Our God has a special plan, purpose, and people for Jerusalem. Listen to Psalm 132:11-14:

> *The LORD hath sworn in truth unto David; he will not turn from it; Of the fruit of thy body will I set upon thy throne. If thy children will keep my covenant and my testimony that I shall teach them, their children shall also sit upon thy throne for evermore. For the LORD hath chosen Zion; he hath desired it for his habitation. This is my rest for ever: here will I dwell; for I have desired it.*

How should we "Pray for Jerusalem"?

1. For the Prince of Peace—Jesus Christ, to come!

> *And from Jesus Christ, who is the faithful witness, and the first begotten of the dead, and the prince of the kings of the earth. Unto him that loved us, and washed us from our sins in his own blood, And hath made us kings and priests unto God and his Father; to him be glory and dominion for ever and ever. Amen. Behold, he cometh with clouds; and every eye shall see him, and they also which pierced him: and all kindreds of the earth shall wail because of him. Even so, Amen* (Rev. 1:5-7).

First, Jesus will come in the rapture (1 Thess. 4:13-18). Then, after the seven years of tribulation on the earth (in heaven the marriage of the lamb takes place), Jesus will come again as described in Luke 21:24-28.

2. For the Prince of Peace—Jesus Christ, to come and build His tem-

ple! (Ezek. 40-48)

> *And the glory of the Lord came into the house by the way of the gate whose prospect is toward the east. So the spirit took me up, and brought me into the inner court; and, behold, the glory of the Lord filled the house (Ezek. 43:4-5).*

What a description of Messiah's Temple! All the other temples—inluding Herod's, do not compare to this Millennial Temple.

3. For the Prince of Peace—Jesus Christ, to come set up His kingdom!

> *I saw in the night visions, and, behold, one like the Son of man came with the clouds of heaven, and came to the Ancient of days, and they brought him near before him. And there was given him dominion, and glory, and a kingdom, that all people, nations, and languages, should serve him: his dominion is an everlasting dominion, which shall not pass away, and his kingdom that which shall not be destroyed (Dan. 7:13-14).*

Jesus Christ will have authority and dominion during the Kingdom period on earth, which is yet to come.

4. For the Prince of Peace—Jesus Christ, to come set up His Kingdom and rule and reign!

> *And I saw thrones, and they sat upon them, and judgment was given unto them: and I saw the souls of them that were beheaded for the witness of Jesus, and for the word of God, and which had not worshipped the beast, neither his image, neither had received his mark upon their foreheads, or in their hands; and they lived and reigned with Christ a thousand years. But the rest of the*

> *dead lived not again until the thousand years were finished. This is the first resurrection. Blessed and holy is he that hath part in the first resurrection: on such the second death hath no power, but they shall be priests of God and of Christ, and shall reign with him a thousand years* (Rev. 20:4-6).

Satan's bound. Martyrs resurrected. Jesus enthroned.

5. For the Prince of Peace—Jesus Christ, to come set up His Kingdom and then create the New Jerusalem, in which we will live forever!

> *And I saw no temple therein: for the Lord God Almighty and the Lamb are the temple of it. And the city had no need of the sun, neither of the moon, to shine in it: for the glory of God did lighten it, and the Lamb is the light thereof. And the nations of them which are saved shall walk in the light of it: and the kings of the earth do bring their glory and honour into it. And the gates of it shall not be shut at all by day: for there shall be no night there. And they shall bring the glory and honour of the nations into it. And there shall in no wise enter into it any thing that defileth, neither whatsoever worketh abomination, or maketh a lie: but they which are written in the Lamb's book of life* (Rev. 21:22-27).

The New Jerusalem is waiting in the future for us! What about it?

Conclusion: No wonder the Psalmist instructs us to *"Pray for the peace of Jerusalem: they shall prosper that love thee."* In light of what is transpiring today in Jerusalem—let's pray.

> *Thy kingdom come, Thy will be done in earth, as it is in heaven* (Matt. 6:10).

WHERE TO GO IN TIME OF NEED

Introduction: When a tornado, hurricane, or deadly virus hits, we need "Disaster Relief"! Everybody needs a place to go "In Time of Need." Do you have a place? Where do you go? After declaring the superiority of Jesus Christ over angels, Moses, and the old covenant, the writer of Hebrews (I believe Paul) discusses the dominating theme of the letter—entering into rest and coming to the "Throne of Grace." Two parts seem evident: Who can we go to IN TIME OF NEED? And, where can we go to IN TIME OF NEED?

> *Seeing then that we have a great high priest, that is passed into the heavens, Jesus the Son of God, let us hold fast our profession. For we have not an high priest which cannot be touched with the feeling of our infirmities; but was in all points tempted like as we are, yet without sin. Let us therefore come boldly unto the throne of grace, that we may obtain mercy, and find grace to help in time of need* (Heb. 4:14-16).

- Jesus our great high priest passed beyond us (v. 14).
- Jesus our high priest understands us (v. 15).

1. Who can we go to IN TIME OF NEED?

    > *Seeing then that we have a great high priest, that is passed into the heavens, Jesus the Son of God, let us hold fast our profession. For we have not an high priest which cannot be touched with the feeling of our infirmities; but was in all points tempted like as we are, yet without sin* (v. 14-15).

2. Where can we go IN TIME OF NEED?

    > *Let us therefore come boldly unto the throne of grace, that we*

may obtain mercy, and find grace to help in time of need (v. 16).

- Invited to God's throne of grace.
- Mercy and grace to help IN TIME OF NEED.

Conclusion: It brings great comfort and peace to our hearts to know, "Who we can go to and where we can we go to IN TIME OF NEED!" When we go to God's throne of grace...

- Burdens are lifted.
- Grace is given.
- Peace is imparted.
- Breakthroughs are experienced.
- Strength is sent.
- Rest is found.
- Jesus is there.

Come on... Let's go to "God's Throne of Grace."

HOW TO TAKE A LOAD OFF

Introduction: Do you feel like you are carrying a LOAD? Load of CARE? What is it you are troubled over today? Is it consuming your mind and energy? How can we deal with "CARE" without it dealing with us? Peter understood the significance of facing hardships and sufferings; and yet he was led by the Holy Spirit to give us some instructions as to "what to do" during those experiences. In his epistle, First Peter, he covers a number of both spiritual and practical "truths that transform."

Suffering of the strangers scattered (1 Pet. 1).
Suffering of the Savior and our Substitute (1 Pet. 2).
Suffering and the Scriptures for the skeptic (1 Pet. 3).
Suffering for the saints for not singing (1 Pet. 4).
Suffering and struggling under stress (1 Pet. 5).

1. Lay all your TROUBLES DOWN!

   Humble yourselves therefore under the mighty hand of God, that he may exalt you in due time: Casting all your care upon him; for he careth for you (1 Pet. 5:6-7).

   - The word *"humble"* (Greek–tapinoo) means to make low, reduce, lower rank, down one's pride, lower one's opinion of self.
   - The word *"exalt"* (Greek–hoopsoo) means to lift up on high.
   - The word *"cast"* (Greek–epirhripto) means throw, place.
   - The word *"care"* (Greek–merimnan) means distraction, anxiety.

Are you distracted? Will you humble yourself? How much care are you carrying? Throw it down!

2. Lay all your TROUBLES DOWN upon the Lord Jesus!

   For he careth for you... (1 Pet. 5:7).

   - The word *"care"* (Greek - melo) means "cares about."

Doesn't it bring comfort and peace to your heart to know that our God CARES for US? After all, He knows us!

   Conclusion: Decision time... Are we going to continue to carry our cares around until they drag us down (mentally, emotionally, spiritually—breakdown)? Or will we "THROW" our anxieties on Jesus because not only does He CARE for us, but PRAISE GOD—He can carry them as well.

   - He loves us.
   - He cares for us.
   - He bought us.
   - He's gone to prepare a place for us.
   - He's coming back for us.

Take a LOAD off!

WHEN THE FIRE FALLS

Introduction: Are there a lot of false prophets today? It seems like many are boasting to have special revelation as well as predicting events to happen that never do. In Elijah's day, there were quite a few false prophets. However, Elijah was a man of prayer; also, he trusted in the God of the Bible. Yet, his FAITH was constantly being tested.

Does God answer all prayers? One preacher described answers to every prayer in this manner. "If the request is wrong, God says NO! If the timing is not right, God says SLOW. If we are not right, God says GROW. But if the request is right, the timing is right, and we are right, God says GO!"

In Elijah's case, God says GO!

> *And Elijah came unto all the people, and said, How long halt ye between two opinions? if the LORD be God, follow him: but if Baal, then follow him* (1 Kings 18:21).

1. When the fire falls, the devil's crowd is HORRIFIED!

> *And Elijah said unto them, Take the prophets of Baal; let not one of them escape. And they took them: and Elijah brought them down to the brook Kishon, and slew them there* (1 Kings 18:40).

2. When the fire falls, the saints are PURIFIED!

> *And when all the people saw it, they fell on their faces: and they said, The LORD, he is the God; the LORD, he is the God* (1 Kings 18:39).

3. When the fire falls, the Lord is GLORIFIED!

> *Hear me, O LORD, hear me, that this people may know that thou art the LORD God, and that thou hast turned their heart back again. Then the fire of the LORD fell and consumed the burnt sacrifice, and the wood, and the stones, and the dust, and licked up the water that was in the trench* (1 Kings 18:37-38).

Conclusion: Interestingly enough, this was not Elijah's first test. In fact, in the previous chapter, he was instructed to go to a brook to be fed by ravens. The brook dried up, and he was led by the Lord to be a blessing to a widow woman and her son. All of this was preparation for the bigger battles of FAITH. He prayed for the heavens to be shut from sending forth the rain, and the windows of heaven were closed. Three and half years later, he lifted his voice to the throne of GRACE and the result was a torrential downpour. James claims that we have like passions as Elijah. Therefore, the same great and mighty God that answered by fire in Elijah's dilemma is the same Sovereign Lord of today.

We can trust Him! Let's pray and expect the "spiritual fire" to fall.

PRAY YOUR WORRIES AWAY

Introduction: Have you been worrying lately? We are all facing multiple ANXIETIES (family, finances, future) and are tempted to WORRY because we can't control everything. The word "worry" or "anxiety" is merimnao, which pictures a dog leaping into the air going for the jugular vein. If doctors could invent a WORRY-FREE pill, it would almost empty the hospitals. A few years ago these statistics were revealed:

- 40% of the things we WORRY about never happen... that's almost half!
- of the 40%, only 8% are legitimate concerns!

NEWSFLASH—Doctor Jesus has a cure! Paul explains...

1. Why be WORRIED with CARE, when we can be blessed with PRAYER?

> *Be careful for nothing; but in everything by prayer and supplication...* (Phil. 4:6).

The word *"careful"* means full of care.

The definition of worry:

- Mental disorder
- Low grade fever
- Pulling apart of the mind
- Dividing the mind

According to statistics:

- 1 in 8 Americans between the ages of 18 years old and 63 years old are plagued with ANXIETY.
- ANXIETY is the #1 issue with those 65 years and older.

2. Why should we be unthankful and depressed, when we can have God's SWEET PEACE and REST?

> *With thanksgiving let your request be known to God. And the peace of God, which passeth all understanding, shall keep your hearts and minds through Christ Jesus* (Phil. 4:6-7).

The word *"peace"* is eirene, which means a state of tranquility. The word *"keep"* is phroureo, which means guard, protect, to prevent a hostile invasion. Don't you love that!

- Peace that surpasses.
- Peace that protects.

Conclusion: Worry is a person with a bended head, carrying a load of feathers, but thinks it's lead. Why pray when you can worry? Or better yet, why worry when you can pray? One lady named Betty Phillips used to tell me in jest, I'm WORRIED that I'm not WORRIED"! You ask, so how does this biblical principle work?

Simply put—when we take our eyes off our seemingly insurmountable problems, i.e., cares and worries, which cause anxieties, and instead talk to God, our focus becomes how big and mighty He is in comparison to our situation or feelings. Consequently, our trust in Him releases a state of rest (a guard around our hearts and minds)—something we can't explain. So rather than WORRY with CARE, we can be blessed with PRAYER, and instead of being depressed, we can experience our Lord's PEACE and SWEET REST. Praise the Lord!

NOT MY WILL

Introduction: I visited a lady who was dying and she knew it. After being told by the doctors there was nothing else they could do, she was overwhelmed with fear. Unable to come to peace, she expressed to me when I visited her, that she was terrified with anxiety. At that moment our Lord impressed upon my heart to ask her if she had ever prayed this prayer, "Not my will, but thine, oh Lord!" Honestly, acknowledging she had not, she prayed out loud right then and there, "Not my will, but yours Lord Jesus be done." Immediately, a sense of peace and tranquility came over her face. She relaxed and took a deep breath. The next day while visiting her, I asked her if she was afraid of dying. She smiled and said, "Not my will but His will." The next day she was with Jesus in heaven. I stood around the bedside with her husband of over fifty years. We cried but rejoiced. She made it to her new home—in heaven with Jesus.

You know, Jesus prayed that prayer—have you? Lately?

1. If you pray it and mean it, it will relieve you from trying to be in control!

> *Saying, Father, if thou be willing, remove this cup from me: nevertheless not my will, but thine, be done* (Luke 22:42).

Feeling alone with the weight of the world's sin upon his shoulders, literally—Jesus was not afraid of dying, but rather of "tasting sin" or experiencing hell (separation from the Father). And yet, He drank the cup to the last bitter dregs. He did it for me! Us! That we would not have to be separated from the Father.

2. If you pray it and mean it, this will release you from things you cannot control!

> *And he came out, and went, as he was wont, to the mount of Olives; and his disciples also followed him. And when he was at the place, he said unto them, Pray that ye enter not into temptation. And he was withdrawn from them about a stone's cast, and kneeled down, and prayed, Saying, Father, if thou be willing, remove this cup from me: nevertheless not my will, but thine, be done. And there appeared an angel unto him from heaven, strengthening him* (Luke 22:39-43).

After sweating great drops of blood from intensity, an angel strengthened Jesus. Praise the Lord for the ministry of angels!

3. If you pray it and mean it, it will help you resolve that God is in control!

> *And being in an agony he prayed more earnestly: and his sweat was as it were great drops of blood falling down to the ground. And when he rose up from prayer, and was come to his disciples, he found them sleeping for sorrow, And said unto them, Why sleep ye? rise and pray, lest ye enter into temptation* (Luke 22:44-46).

God the Father's will is the most important part of the believer's life. Although we like to be in control, the sooner we relinquish control—the better off we will be.

Conclusion: I shared the aforementioned account of the Christian lady with another Christian lady who had been diagnosed with a terminal illness. Sensing her time was coming to an end, she too prayed... "Not my will, but your will be done." Will you pray that now? "Not my will Lord Jesus, but your will be done"! Jesus—though He was God in the flesh, prayed, *"Father, if thou be willing, remove this cup from me: nevertheless not my will, but thine, be done."* Amen.

PRAYER AND FASTING

FASTING FOR FREEDOM

Introduction: Are you distracted? Does your mind wander? Is it difficult to concentrate? When PRAYING do other things consume your thought processes? Why? What can you do? Is there help? How can this lack of concentration be overcome? Have you ever tried PRAYER and FASTING?

If this was not important, Jesus would not have emphasized it. Do you agree?

1. For starters, WHAT did Jesus teach about FASTING in the context of PRAYER?

Moreover when ye fast, be not, as the hypocrites, of a sad countenance: for they disfigure their faces, that they may appear unto men to fast. Verily I say unto you, They have their reward (Matt. 6:16).

Speaking to His disciples about "HOW" and "WHAT" to PRAY, Jesus gives similar instructions on FASTING. Notice He says, "WHEN you FAST," not IF you FAST!

This is in the context of that great model PRAYER:

After this manner therefore pray ye: Our Father which art in heaven, Hallowed be thy name. Thy kingdom come. Thy will be done in earth, as it is in heaven. Give us this day our daily bread. And forgive us our debts, as we forgive our debtors. And lead us not into temptation, but deliver us from evil: For thine is the kingdom, and the power, and the glory, for ever. Amen (Matt. 6:9-14).

It becomes abundantly clear that PRAYER and FASTING go together. Check out all the biblical saints who practiced PRAYER and FASTING including our Lord Jesus. My conclusion—it must be important.

2. Next, HOW did JESUS instruct His disciples to FAST?

But thou, when thou fastest, anoint thine head, and wash thy face; That thou appear not unto men to fast, but unto thy Father which is in secret: and thy Father, which seeth in secret, shall reward thee openly (Matt. 6:17-18).

The believer's motive for FASTING is exactly the same for PRAYING. Do it in secret! Of course, this does not negate public PRAYING. Our Lord Jesus did that as well. But the point is do not do either one for "show" or the approval of men. Instead, spend TIME with our FATHER in secret, and He will REWARD you.

By the way, the PURPOSE for PRAYER and FASTING is not just to get what we NEED, but to get in FELLOWSHIP with our CREATOR... in tune, in step, and in touch with Him. How are you doing in this area? Do you need to re-evaluate your motives?

Conclusion: As mentioned in the introduction, when we FAST and PRAY with the right motives, things happen that would not happen ordinarily. Try it. You will like it. But more importantly, Jesus will like it and BLESS it!

FASTING FOR FOCUS

Introduction: If fasting was good for Jesus, it seems good to me! Although we are not Jesus Christ—we are to follow Him, submit to Him, obey Him, and allow Him to live in us through His Spirit—as we are conformed to His image. Knowing what lay ahead in His earthly ministry, Jesus was prompted to start off by FASTING—40 days and 40 nights—a supernatural fast!

> *Then was Jesus led up of the Spirit into the wilderness to be tempted of the devil. And when he had fasted forty days and forty nights, he was afterward an hungred* (Matt. 4:1-2).

Check it out:

1. The Living Word used the written Word against the devil while fasting!

> *And when the tempter came to him, he said, If thou be the Son of God, command that these stones be made bread. But he answered and said, It is written, Man shall not live by bread alone, but by every word that proceedeth out of the mouth of God* (Matt. 4:3-4).

Imagine the hunger pangs. Satan hits us when we are weak, and where we are strong. But as we "fine tune" our spiritual senses, the flesh decreases while the Spirit increases! It is amazing how that works!! Could you use a little more of the Spirit? Spiritual power?

2. The Living Word used the written Word to overcome the world, the flesh, and the devil while fasting!

> *And saith unto him, If thou be the Son of God, cast thyself down:*

> *for it is written, He shall give his angels charge concerning thee: and in their hands they shall bear thee up, lest at any time thou dash thy foot against a stone. Jesus said unto him, It is written again, Thou shalt not tempt the Lord thy God* (Matt. 4:6-7).

Temptation comes knocking on our door. Do you know what to do? Send Jesus to the door! Is the devil tempting you to sin against God? Lean on your own understanding? Take credit? What should you do? Pray. Fast as the Spirit leads.

3. The Living Word through the written Word becomes the fleshed out Word while Fasting!

> *Again, the devil taketh him up into an exceeding high mountain, and sheweth him all the kingdoms of the world, and the glory of them; And saith unto him, All these things will I give thee, if thou wilt fall down and worship me. Then saith Jesus unto him, Get thee hence, Satan: for it is written, Thou shalt worship the Lord thy God, and him only shalt thou serve. Then the devil leaveth him, and, behold, angels came and ministered unto him* (Matt. 4:8-11).

Do you want to get rid of the devil's accusations and temptations? Try fasting and praying. Did you notice how our Lord exercised power over the enemy?

   Conclusion: Our power to overcome the devil is through the power of Jesus Christ. Yet, since He demonstrated the value of prayer and fasting, it is a lesson for those of us who follow Him. Do you want to be an overcomer? Fast for focus!

FASTING FOR THE FAMILY

Introduction: Does your family need a "BREAKTHROUGH"? Try fasting....of course with the right motives and for the right purpose. When Ezra and the people of God were rejoicing because of the GOODNESS of the Lord, they were also needing His BLESSINGS for what was ahead. Truthfully, we can all relate! Check out and see if you are led to "FAST for the FAMILY."

1. Fasting for focusing on your family!

> *Then I proclaimed a fast there, at the river of Ahava, that we might afflict ourselves before our God, to seek of him a right way for us, and for our little ones, and for all our substance* (Ezra 8:21).

Here is the burden—our families—*"our little ones."* Every family has spiritual needs. Some of these needs will only be met through prayer and fasting. Such was the case throughout the Bible (see Mark 9:14-29). Is your family worth it? Is God's glory worth it? While no one may ever know of your time spent in secret alone with Jesus—He knows! That's all that really matters!!

2. Fasting for fighting our foes!

> *For I was ashamed to require of the king a band of soldiers and horsemen to help us against the enemy in the way: because we had spoken unto the king, saying, The hand of our God is upon all them for good that seek him; but his power and his wrath is against all them that forsake him. So we fasted and besought our God for this: and he was intreated of us... Then we departed from the river of Ahava on the twelfth day of the first month, to go unto Jerusalem: and the hand of our God was upon us, and*

he delivered us from the hand of the enemy, and of such as lay in wait by the way (Ezra 8:22-23, 31).

In this case, fasting released God's restraining power over Israel's enemy. We can conclude that our Lord heard His people's cry and honored their sacrificial faith directed to Him. Is Jesus the same today? Yes! *"Jesus Christ the same yesterday, and to day, and for ever"* (Heb. 13:8).

Conclusion: Will you take time to FAST for your FAMILY? Let our Lord lead you to what kind of FAST; i.e. skipping a meal or two, tv, computer, etc. Watch what Jesus will do because of His FAITHFULNESS.

FASTING FOR YOUR FAITH

Introduction: Have you ever felt spiritually dull? Apathetic? Complacent? Does the world ever pull you down? Do you feel vexed? Worn out? Tired? Distracted? What should you do? Try fasting. Both a national crisis, as well as a spiritual crisis, calls for fasting. The prophet Joel saw the vision.

1. God's call to His people to FAST and pray because of a national crisis!

The nation of Israel was under God's judgment because of their idolatry. But there was HOPE.

> *For a nation is come up upon my land, strong, and without number, whose teeth are the teeth of a lion, and he hath the cheek teeth of a great lion* (Joel 1:6).

Our Lord would use the Assyrians to invade the northern kingdom called Israel in 722 BC. But listen to the prophet's call.

> *Gird yourselves, and lament, ye priests: howl, ye ministers of the altar: come, lie all night in sackcloth, ye ministers of my God: for the meat offering and the drink offering is withholden from the house of your God. Sanctify ye a fast, call a solemn assembly, gather the elders and all the inhabitants of the land into the house of the LORD your God, and cry unto the LORD* (Joel 1:13-14).

God's remedy for chastisement is FASTING and PRAYER... which results in returning to Him.

2. God's call to His people to FAST and pray because of a spiritual crisis!

> *Therefore also now, saith the LORD, turn ye even to me with all your heart, and with fasting, and with weeping, and with mourning: And rend your heart, and not your garments, and turn unto the LORD your God: for he is gracious and merciful, slow to anger, and of great kindness, and repenteth him of the evil* (Joel 2:12-13).

Brokenness leads to BLESSINGS! Our Lord is gracious and merciful. When we repent and return to Jesus with fasting and prayer, He forgives our sin and restores us to fellowship. Listen to the words of Joel:

> *Blow the trumpet in Zion, sanctify a fast, call a solemn assembly: Gather the people, sanctify the congregation, assemble the elders, gather the children, and those that suck the breasts: let the bridegroom go forth of his chamber, and the bride out of her closet. Let the priests, the ministers of the LORD, weep between the porch and the altar, and let them say, Spare thy people, O LORD, and give not thine heritage to reproach, that the heathen should rule over them: wherefore should they say among the people, Where is their God?* (Joel 2:15-17).

Did you notice how many times God calls His people to FAST and return?

3. God will answer His people as they FAST and pray and return to Him!

> *Then will the LORD be jealous for his land, and pity his people. Yea, the LORD will answer and say unto his people, Behold, I will send you corn, and wine, and oil, and ye shall be satisfied therewith: and I will no more make you a reproach among the heathen* (Joel 2:18-19).

God is faithful! As He calls us to seek Him—He responds. Will you seek Him today?

Conclusion: We live in a sin-sick world. Our nation has defied the true and living God. The Lord has no other alternative but to bring more judgment on America. Yet, He will pardon and restore truth and righteousness as we FAST and Pray for His BLESSINGS! Yes—He will, at least within the hearts of His people. Let's do it!!

FASTING AND FAITHFUL SERVICE

Introduction: What does fasting have to do with faith? Take a moment to look at this godly woman who demonstrated how we can live a life that pleases our Lord.

1. A life well lived with the practice of PRAYER and FASTING!

And there was one Anna, a prophetess, the daughter of Phanuel, of the tribe of Aser: she was of a great age, and had lived with an husband seven years from her virginity; And she was a widow of about fourscore and four years, which departed not from the temple, but served God with fastings and prayers night and day (Luke 2:36-37).

Anna was "faithful"! Why? What was her secret? She believed in the power of "prayer and fasting"! Do you?

2. A life well lived with the practice of PRAYER and FASTING made her a great WITNESS and WORSHIPPER!

And she coming in that instant gave thanks likewise unto the Lord, and spake of him to all them that looked for redemption in Jerusalem (Luke 2:38).

When our spiritual focus is refined it redirects our calling and purpose in life. No longer are we focused on the minors, but instead on the majors. Eternity is in sight. God's will is supreme. Pleasing Him is our goal. Living for self fades away.

Conclusion: Fasting is a tool our Lord uses to mold us into a useable vessel. Keeping the main thing the main thing is the key! Jesus Christ is the main thing. His will and purpose is utmost. Prayer and fasting can keep us on track.

BREAKTHROUGHS OVER STRONGHOLDS

Introduction: Do you need a BREAKTHROUGH over a stronghold? A "stronghold" (Greek-ochyroma) is a "castle, a fortress." All of us deal with unwanted generational "baggages" such as anger, bitterness, lust, self-righteousness, fantasies, greed, temporary escapism-inability to cope with stress and life, etc. These can manifest thru unfulfilled needs, a lack of a healthy God-given self image, and an absence of God's truth. How can we as believers OVERCOME these strongholds? Mark, the secretary of Peter, gives us four steps to experience a BREAKTHROUGH:

1. We, like the disciples, have to deal with being DEFEATED and DISCOURAGED!

After a heavenly, mountaintop {transfiguration} experience with Jesus, the disciples are confronted with a demon-possessed boy whose dad was trying to get him help.

> *Master, I have brought unto thee my son which hath a dumb spirit... I spake to thy disciples that they should cast him out; and they could not* (Mark 9:17-18).

- Disciples defeated
- Prayerless Christians = Powerless

> *The disciples asked him privately, Why could not we cast him out?... And he said unto them, This kind can come forth by nothing, but by prayer and fasting* (Mark 9:28-29).

2. We, like the daddy, have to deal with being DOWN in the DUMPS!

Jesus asked the father, "How long is it ago since this came unto him? And he said, Of a child." And the DOUBTING DADDY said, "If thou canst do anything, have compassion on us, and help us" (Mark 9:21-24).

- Doubt and do without.
- Doubt turned into desperation.

The father cried out... with tears, Lord I believe; help thou mine unbelief (Mark 9:24).

The word "HELP" in verse 22 means instant but "HELP" in verse 24 means continuous.

3. We, like the DEFEATED disciples and the DOUBTING daddy, have to deal with DEADLY DEMONS!

Speaking of the demon, the dad said,

....he taketh him, he teareth: and he foameth, and gnasheth with his teeth, and pineth away (Mark 9:18-20).

- The Strongman's Stronghold.
- Deadly demon's destroying—convulses, shrieks, wasting away.

4. We need to let the DIVINE DELIVERER DELIVER!

Bring him to me.... if thou canst believe, all things are possible to him that believeth.... I charge thee, come out of him (Mark 9:19, 23, 25).

- Get people to JESUS.

- Demons must obey.

Conclusion: Strongholds are real.... but they must SUBMIT to the STRONGER One—JESUS! Whether you believe it or not, I experienced a demon-possessed lady on the mission field in the interior of Guyana (way in the backwoods only accessible by boat). Her mother brought her to me, asking for help; this was after preaching one night... everybody (about 100 village people) had left.... the demon-possessed lady growled like a wild animal and shrieked and shrilled at the top of her lungs! Her eyes were sunk in the back of her head. At first, I was looking for a BACK DOOR! Then, our Lord reminded me about HIS wonder-working power thru His BLOOD, His WORD, & HIS NAME! After praying and trusting in HIM for deliverance, she was set FREE! Her countenance changed!! Her voice returned normal and we REJOICED in what a Mighty GOD we SERVE! She had a "BREAKTHROUGH over a STRONGHOLD"!

A HEART CRY TURNS INTO HOUSEHOLD SALVATION

Introduction: Does prayer work? Can Jesus save someone through prayer? Will you pray for someone who is not a CHRISTian today? Cornelius was a seeker of God but not quite a "Sealed and Saved Servant" of the Lord. He was PRAYING and FASTING with the light he had (he was not born again at the time). But his conversion came about by a believer in Jesus Christ who was also PRAYING and FASTING, namely, Peter. God the Holy Spirit hunted down Cornelius and captured his heart along with his whole family.

You see, God was working on both ends—on Cornelius and on Peter—to orchestrate His will. Please take note how it was accomplished.

1. When God the Holy Spirit is working on one end!

> *There was a certain man in Caesarea called Cornelius, a centurion of the band called the Italian band, A devout man, and one that feared God with all his house, which gave much alms to the people, and prayed to God alway. He saw in a vision evidently about the ninth hour of the day an angel of God coming in to him, and saying unto him, Cornelius. And when he looked on him, he was afraid, and said, What is it, Lord? And he said unto him, Thy prayers and thine alms are come up for a memorial before God. And now send men to Joppa, and call for one Simon, whose surname is Peter:* (Acts 10:1-5).

Although Cornelius was a God-fearing man, yet he had not heard the gospel of Jesus Christ... that He died for our sins on a cross, arose victoriously from the grave, and offers forgiveness and eternal life through faith and trust in Him. The bottom line: Cornelius was obeying the light that he had, but desperately needed more light!

Prayer is a cycle which circles from earth (birthed by the Holy Spirit in the hearts of people). Prayer ascends to heaven where Jesus sits on the right hand of the Father making intercession for us. As our Great High Priest, He answers the prayers according to His will and purpose—then sends the answers back to earth however He chooses. Does hearing this make you want to pray more?

This leads us to discover how the Lord answered this "Heart Cry" from Cornelius. And then we can witness the lesson Peter learned about sharing the "GOSPEL" to the unclean race called the Gentiles. Do you believe the "GOSPEL" is still the power of God unto salvation?

2. When God the Holy Spirit is working on the other end!

> *On the morrow, as they went on their journey, and drew nigh unto the city, Peter went up upon the housetop to pray about the sixth hour: And he became very hungry, and would have eaten: but while they made ready, he fell into a trance, And saw heaven opened, and a certain vessel descending unto him, as it had been a great sheet knit at the four corners, and let down to the earth: Wherein were all manner of fourfooted beasts of the earth, and wild beasts, and creeping things, and fowls of the air. And there came a voice to him, Rise, Peter; kill, and eat. But Peter said, Not so, Lord; for I have never eaten any thing that is common or unclean. And the voice spake unto him again the second time, What God hath cleansed, that call not thou common. This was done thrice: and the vessel was received up again into heaven* (Acts 10:9-16).

Did you notice that Peter was obedient to the Holy Spirit? In fact, even before he was directed to go and preach the gospel to Cornelius, he was spending time—daily disciplines—with his Lord. That was the key to him being used by the Holy Spirit. Don't you want to be used for God's glory? Just when you think someone will not or cannot be saved—our Lord surprises everyone. Aren't you glad that He did not give up on YOU! Praise the Lord!!

Please pay attention to how God works to save a whole family. Can He still do it today? Yes!

3. Household Salvation occurs!

> *While Peter thought on the vision, the Spirit said unto him, Behold, three men seek thee. Arise therefore, and get thee down, and go with them, doubting nothing: for I have sent them. Then Peter went down to the men which were sent unto him from Cornelius; and said, Behold, I am he whom ye seek: what is the cause wherefore ye are come?... While Peter yet spake these words, the Holy Ghost fell on all them which heard the word. And they of the circumcision which believed were astonished, as many as came with Peter, because that on the Gentiles also was poured out the gift of the Holy Ghost* (Acts 10:19-21, 44-45).

If we are going to see the conversions of people—we must be led by the Holy Spirit. Think with me for a moment... Jesus knows "where" people are in relation to Him and "how" to get them to His WORD in order to SAVE them through His REDEEMING blood.

Grant it. He can do it without us, yet He chooses to use us because of His great LOVE. Don't you want others to experience FREEDOM from the penalty of sin, the power of sin, and ultimately the presence of sin?

4. How God the Holy Spirit brought it all together!

And Cornelius said, Four days ago I was fasting until this hour; and at the ninth hour I prayed in my house, and, behold, a man stood before me in bright clothing, And said, Cornelius, thy prayer is heard, and thine alms are had in remembrance in the sight of God (Acts 10:30-31).

Did you hear that? The Lord REMEMBERS. He has not forgotten you or me! He REMEMBERS our tears, our needs, and our prayers for others. Doesn't that BLESS you?

Conclusion: Who do you need to pray for right now? Will you do it? Don't procrastinate. Follow through. Try PRAYER and FASTING. Be ready to join the greatest work on earth through the power of the Holy Spirit—converting men, women, boys, and girls to faith in Jesus Christ.

There is a CROWN of REJOICING awaiting at the Judgment Seat of Christ. See you there!

CHAPTER FIVE
THE INTERCESSOR'S PRAYER

*Likewise the Spirit also helpeth our infirmities:
for we know not what we should pray for as we ought:
but the Spirit itself maketh intercession for us
with groanings which cannot be uttered.*

Romans 8:26

It pays to pray beforehand! When it comes to witnessing and sharing the gospel that Jesus died for our sins, arose from the grave, and is coming back again—prayer must be a priority. With this in mind, let me share a couple of personal experiences.

PRAYER FOR A LOST FAMILY MEMBER

A few years ago on a Sunday night, a dear Christian lady and her faithful husband came to the altar to pray. Feeling impressed by the Holy Spirit, I joined them. Her heart cry went something like this... "Dear Lord, I'm concerned for my family member who is not saved. Father, speak to Viola and change her heart. Jesus we know you love her and died for her sins and desire to make her your child."

As we agreed in prayer (Matt. 18:19-20), it became obvious that at her aunt's age (91), time was running out. Marcia explained that her

Aunt Viola was really mean—mean as a snake! She would say and do bad things. Through the power of prayer, our Lord birthed an extraordinary faith in our hearts to go and talk with her. Not knowing what to expect, but knowing that our Lord was with us—we drove to her home. Before we arrived, we engaged in a season of prayer to ask for the power of the Holy Spirit to bring conviction and the conversion of her soul... all for the Lord's glory.

After entering her home and chatting with small talk, our Lord moved upon my heart to ask her if she died, where she would spend eternity. She paused—with a blank look on her face. Upon agreeing to listen to what the Bible teaches concerning our choice of two eternal destinies (point blank—heaven or hell), she fell under deep conviction that she was unprepared to meet Jesus. While pressing her on that truth, she was urged to call upon the Lord Jesus to forgive her and save her. Satan made one last effort to keep her from reaching into heaven's glory. She cried out, "Let Marcia pray in my place!" Realizing the enemy's tactic, we prayed through and finally, Viola shouted, "Jesus save me! I have sinned!"

Later, it was confirmed that Jesus had changed her heart. She was born again, heaven-bound, sins forgiven, and made a new creature in Christ. This miraculous transformation happened because of the grace of God released through the vehicle of intercessory prayer. Shortly after that glorious day, she passed away. As I stood before her casket, tears of joy ran down my cheeks. She had been snatched from a devil's hell and translated into the glories of heaven to live forever with the one who redeemed her with His own precious blood.

PRAYER FOR A LOST MAN

Several years ago on a cold January day, we were out knocking on doors in the community. Our goal—to share HOPE with a hopeless world through the love of Jesus Christ.

As we knocked on the door of one home, an old man stuck his head out of the door and started cussing saying, "You ____ - ____ - ____!" Five minutes later, he SLAMMED the door in our face! Feeling REJECTED and HATED, our Lord moved on my heart to wipe the dust off my feet, and pray for mercy for that old, ornery, cantankerous man. Others who lived in the community told me he was a wild man. They spoke of one particular day when he shot his shotgun in the neighborhood to scare people off so they would not come to his house (wish I had known that—not really—Jesus came to save sinners).

Six months passed by until one day a lady called me requesting a hospital visit for an eighty-eight-year-old man who did not have any family anywhere. While purposing in my heart that this might be a divine appointment, I called a Christian brother to go with me to visit him. He prayed for the man while I witnessed to him about how Jesus changed my life.

Upon meeting him, it became obvious that he liked to rabbit hunt. Becoming all things to all men—we engaged in a conversation about hunting. Then the time came when I asked him the question. "If you died today would you go to heaven?" He answered, "No." I asked him if I could share with him what the Bible teaches about how to have a personal relationship with Jesus Christ. He agreed. After reading and quoting numerous Scriptures about how to be saved—he was confronted with the verdict... what he ought to do. He shouted, "I need to be ready to go to heaven!"

I explained that I would pray first for him and then he needed to pray to the God of the Bible and ask for forgiveness of his sins and place his faith and trust in Jesus Christ's shed blood. Oh... the tears that flowed down his cheeks as he cried out to God to forgive him of his many sins. In his prayer he shouted—"Please save me!"

Finally, when he finished praying from his hospital bed—we rejoiced together. The transaction was sealed! Once he was released, he came to church one Sunday and sat in the back. As I was preaching—he stood up and shouted, "That Preacher is going to have a heart attack!!"

Just a few weeks later he passed away. His only friend (he had no family) called me and asked me to preach his funeral at Prospect Methodist Church. With only a handful of people there, our Lord melted my heart to tears as we reflected on how one day—he CUSSED and SLAMMED the door in my face. But, next thing you know, he was in the hospital crying out to Jesus to save his soul.

Certainly our Lord answered the prayers of his only friend as we witnessed the LOVE and GRACE of God in Jesus! I plan to see Mr. Winburn in heaven.

> *But ye, beloved, building up yourselves on your most holy faith, praying in the Holy Ghost, Keep yourselves in the love of God, looking for the mercy of our Lord Jesus Christ unto eternal life. And of some have compassion, making a difference: And others save with fear, pulling them out of the fire; hating even the garment spotted by the flesh* (Jude 20-23).

Have you made that lifelong decision—to trust Jesus Christ as your Lord and Savior? Will you pray for someone right now who does not have a relationship with Jesus Christ? PRAYER WORKS if you WORK it!

CONCLUSION

When a Christian neglects his or her prayer life, there are consequences. I am reminded of the story of the natives. After being gloriously saved, a group of natives began to have daily devotions. The paths were beaten down where they walked daily through the forest to spend time alone at the throne of grace. Then something happened. They stopped spending daily quiet time with God. The grass began to grow up again. Those who saw the grown up paths knew the natives had forsaken their "sweet hour of prayer."

Has the grass grown up on your prayer path? Start walking it again! The Holy Spirit will cut the weeds down, and answered prayer will keep the path clear!

What is needed more than writing or reading a book on PRAYER is engaging in PRAYER. That is this Pastor's ultimate purpose for writing this book. My final remarks about "PRAYER WORKS if you WORK it":

Remember:
- All prayer should glorify our Lord Jesus.
- All prayer should be coupled with FAITH in Jesus.
- All prayer should be offered in Jesus' name.
- All prayer should be given to Jesus with the right motives.
- All prayer should be done with the purpose to develop a closer RELATIONSHIP with Jesus.

Will you join me in PRAYER right now? Then, PRAISE JESUS because... "PRAYER WORKS if you WORK it!"

APPENDIX
A LEGACY OF PRAYER AND FASTING

> The following quotes on prayer and fasting are taken from *Fasting for Spiritual Breakthrough* by Elmer Towns.[1]

"It would not do to say that preachers study too much. Some of them do not study at all; others do not study enough. Numbers do not study the right way to show themselves workmen approved of God. But our great lack is not in head culture, but in heart culture; not in lack of knowledge, but lack of holiness is our sad and telling defect—not that we know too much, but that we do not meditate on God and His Word and watch and fast and pray enough."—*E.M. Bounds*

"I was also led into a state of great dissatisfaction with my own want of stability in faith and love....I often felt myself weak in the presence of temptation and needed frequently to hold days of fasting and prayer and to spend much time in overhauling my own religious life in order to retain that communion with God and that hold upon the Divine truth that would enable me efficiently to labor for the promotion of revivals of religion."—*Charles G. Finney*

"Our ability to perceive God's direction in life is directly related to our ability to sense the inner promptings of His Spirit. God provides a specific activity to assist us in doing this....Men through whom God has worked greatly have emphasized the significance of prayer with fasting....In an extended fast of over three days, one quickly experiences a great decrease in sensual desires and soon has a great new alertness to spiritual things."—*Bill Gothard*

"Fastings and vigils without a special object in view are time run to waste. They are made to minister to a sort of self-gratification, instead of being turned to good account."—*David Livingstone*

"If you say I will fast when God lays it on me, you never will. You are too cold and indifferent. Take the yoke upon you."—*Dwight L. Moody*

"As a Boomer, I have been conditioned to enjoy the best the world has to offer. Fasting speaks boldly to consumerism, one of my generational cover values. To set aside what I want to encourage personal spiritual growth is what it means to deny myself and take up my cross daily in the nineties. I suspect it would be difficult for me to rise to the challenge of discipleship and live a consistently Christian lifestyle without practicing the discipline of fasting."—*Douglas Porter*

"One obvious value of fasting lies in the fact that its discipline helps us keep the body in its place. It is a practical acknowledgement of the supremacy of the spiritual. But in addition to this reflex value, fasting has direct benefits in relation to prayer as well. Many who practice it from right motives and in order to give themselves more unreservedly to prayer testify that the mind becomes unusually clear and vigorous. There are a noticeable spiritual quickening and increased power of concentration on the things of the spirit."—*J. Oswald Sanders*

"We should fast when we are concerned for God's work. I believe the greatest thing a church could have is a staff, deacons, and leaders who fast and pray—not when the church burns down, but in order to get the church on fire. A lot of dead churches would catch fire if the people in places of leadership would set aside a period of time for fasting and prayer....Fasting brings about a supernatural work in our lives. God will not entrust supernatural power to those whose lives are not under total control....The Christian who would have the supernatural power of God must be under the total control of the Holy Spirit.—*Charles Stanley*

"There are those who think that fasting belongs to the old dispensation; but when we look at Acts 14:23 and Acts 13:2-3, we find that it was practiced by the earnest men of the apostolic day. If we would pray with power, we should pray with fasting. This of course, does not mean that we should fast every time we pray; but there are times of emergency or special crisis in work or in our traditional lives, when men of downright earnestness will withdraw themselves even from the gratification of natural appetites that would be perfectly proper under other circumstances, that they may give themselves wholly to prayer. There is a peculiar power in such prayer. Every great crisis in life and work should be met that way. There is nothing pleasing to God in our giving up in a purely Pharasaic and legal way things which are pleasant, but there is power in that downright earnestness and determination to obtain in prayer the things of which we sorely feel our need, that leads us to put away everything, even things in themselves most right and necessary, that we may set our faces to find God, and obtain blessings from Him."—*R.A. Torrey*

"Fasting is important—more important, perhaps, than many of us have supposed, as I trust this book will reveal. For all that, it is not a major biblical doctrine, a foundation stone of the faith, or a panacea for every spiritual ill. Nevertheless, when exercised with a pure heart and a right motive, fasting may provide us with a key to unlock doors where other keys have failed; a window opening up new horizons in the unseen world; a spiritual weapon of God's providing, "mighty, to the pulling down of strongholds." May God use this book to awaken many of His people to all the spiritual possibilities latent in the fast that God has chosen."—*Arthur Wallis*

"A pastor can call for a day of prayer and fasting in his church. Every time I have done this as a pastor we saw unusual results. We usually had it on a Wednesday and closed out with midweek prayer meeting. I would ask the people not to tell me whether or not they were fasting. We would have a special prayer meeting at the church around ten in the morning for those who could come. Some would stay through lunchtime. Sometimes we would break up at noon for the wives who had lunches to prepare of children coming home. An afternoon prayer meeting might be called to be closed out with the evening prayer meeting. Usually a fast would begin in the morning and go to the next morning. That's where the word "breakfast" comes from—it means to "break a fast." There have been times when I fasted only one or two meals in a day because of circumstances."—*C. Summer Wemp*

While prayer doesn't work if you don't work it,
PRAYER WORKS if you WORK IT!

Let's pray!

NOTES

CHAPTER ONE: THE POWER OF PRAYER

1. Charles Haddon Spurgeon, *The Holy Spirit's Intercession* (Metropolitan Tabernacle Pulpit Volume 26, Apr. 11, 1880).

2. Charles Haddon Spurgeon, *The Golden Prayer* (Metropolitan Tabernacle Pulpit Volume 21, Dec. 30, 1877).

CHAPTER TWO: THE PURPOSE OF PRAYER

1. W.A. Criswell, *Criswell Guidebook for Pastors* (B&H Books, 2000).

2. E.M. Bounds, Power Through Prayer (Trinity Press, 2011).

3. C. Peter Wagner, *Prayer Shield* (Chosen Books, 2014).

4. E.M. Bounds, Purpose in Prayer (Baker Publishing, 1978).

CHAPTER THREE: THE POWER OF PRAYER AND FASTING

1. Elmer Towns, *Fasting for Spiritual Breakthrough* (Bethany House Publishers, 2010).

2. Bill Bright, *Seven Steps To Successful Prayer and Fasting* (New Life Publications, 1995).

3. Derek Prince, *Shaping History Through Prayer and Fasting* (Fleming H. Revell Company, 1973).

APPENDIX: A LEGACY OF PRAYER AND FASTING

1. Elmer Towns, *Fasting for Spiritual Breakthrough* (Bethany House Publishers, 2010).

AUTHOR

Dr. Randal Reese is Pastor of New Rocky Creek Baptist Church in Mansfield, Georgia (30+ years), and founder of Until That Day Ministries. Until That Day reaches people with the gospel of Jesus Christ through radio, video, and print media. He and his wife, Deanna, have a son Jeremy, a daughter Beth, a son-in-law Paul, and two granddaughters—Larsen and Karmin.

Contacts:
pastorrandyreese@gmail.com
untilthatdayministries@newrockycreek.org

Education:
B.A. Luther Rice College and Seminary
M.A. Luther Rice College and Seminary
M.Div. Luther Rice College and Seminary
D.Min. Luther Rice College and Seminary, May 2009
Master of Advanced Prophetics,
Louisiana Baptist University, May 2014
Doctor of Philosophy (Ph.D.) of Advanced Prophetics,
Louisiana Baptist University, May 2019

Bible Prophecy Study, Ph.D.
Trip to Israel, Jordan, Turkey, and Rome 2014

Books
Tomorrow's Revelation Calls for Today's Purification, 2016
Church Now Kingdom Later, 2019
Calvinism: Under the Light of Scripture, 2021
Prayer Works If You Work It, 2022

Until That Day Radio Ministry
WJGA Jackson, Georgia (2017 to present)
WDYN Chattanooga, Tennessee (2017 to present)

Until That Day Online Ministry
YouTube Channel — www.youtube.com/untilthatday
Facebook Page — www.facebook.com/untilthatdayministries

A STUDY OF BIBLE PROPHECY FROM GENESIS TO REVELATION

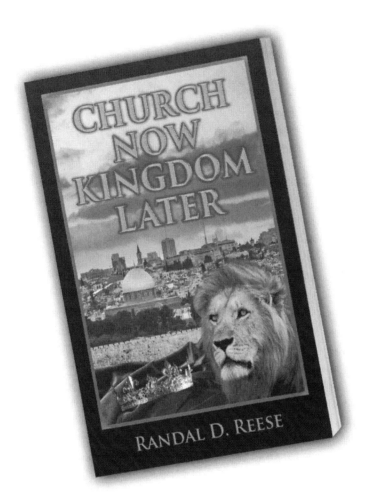

IS THE KINGDOM NOW? OR IS IT LATER?

There are those who claim the church is now in the kingdom. Are there enough biblical evidences to justify this position? Conversely, there are those who teach the kingdom is yet to come in a futuristic event. Can both be correct? Does the Bible indicate which is true?

Available for purchase online.

STOP LOOKING DOWN AND START LOOKING UP!

PREPARE FOR HIS GLORIOUS COMING

"Given the current world events, it is incumbent on the believer to know what God is up to in the world both now and in the future. Dr. Reese aptly describes how we as Christians should order our steps to be prepared and purified." ~James Flanagan, Ph.D., President Emeritus, Luther Rice College and Seminary

Available for purchase online.

VISIT THE UNTIL THAT DAY YOUTUBE CHANNEL

OVER 100 VIDEOS ON BIBLE PROPHECY

Until That Day provides on time truth you can trust. The Word of God speaks of an increase in false teaching and deception in the latter days. Pastor and teacher, Dr. Randal Reese, is committed to teaching the truth of the Word of God—without apology and without compromise. New videos uploaded weekly!

Visit www.youtube.com/untilthatday